FARMGIRL SCHOOL

Homesteading 101:

Back to Basics for an Enchanting, Simple Life

By Katie Lynn Sanders

Table of Contents

FORWORD

Dear Reader,

This book is made up of excerpts from my blog, Farmgirlschool.org. It all started as a journal of our triumphs and failures and learned as we went. We were like many folks out there who were never taught these skills and didn't grow up in this lifestyle so we had to start from scratch. From chicken scratch! We had to learn how much to water, what to plant, how to take care of a chicken and how the heck to milk a goat! Now eat our own vegetables and fruits, work for ourselves, farm our yard at our newly purchased home and love every second of our freedom from the corporate and modern world.

What life there is in homesteading! Choosing your own schedule, being close to nature, and breathing in every moment of healthy work and play is what homesteading is all about. Not to mention the great security in knowing you are caring for yourself and your loved ones and are not near as reliant on big companies.

When the blog started we were living on two thirds of an acre in a small town with our children and each year we learned and chronicled valuable skills and lessons as we made our way to our dream homestead. Most of the articles were written from our small town home. In the fall of 2014 we moved to an old 1905 homestead in Calhan, Colorado that sits on ten acres overlooking the majestic valleys and mountains from our perch on the high plains.

We have since moved on from there, having lived in friends' homes, to and apartment in the city to where we are now.

We now own our own urban homestead in the city of Pueblo. We have a double-lot a block away from a lake in a city park, and we plan to turn the whole thing into gardens and orchards and chicken pens!

This book will take you through the first two years of our never-ending journey, so, whether you want to homestead in the city or leave the workforce to become a farmer, may this book give you a bit more insight on how to do things so you don't have to start quite from the beginning as we did!

Here's to the good life, Folks. See you 'round the farm.

-Katie

Part 1 (Becoming a Homesteader, Living the life you want)

What Is A Homestead?

"What is a homestead?" my friend asked. The question threw me off guard, cause, geez, everyone knows what a homestead is. It's uh....you know...a place where...I decided to consult the dictionary.

homestead

[hohm-sted, -stid] /'hoʊm stɛd, -stɪd/

noun

1. A dwelling with its land and buildings, occupied by the owner as a home and exempted by a homestead law from seizure or sale for debt.

2. Any dwelling with its land and buildings where a family makes its home.

3. A tract of land acquired under the Homestead Act.

4. A house in an urban area acquired under a homesteading program.

Verb (used with object)

1. To acquire or settle on (land) as a homestead:

Pioneers homesteaded the valley.

Verb (used without object)

2. To acquire or settle on a homestead:

They homesteaded many years ago.

And that, my friends, did not help me either because, frankly, I don't own anything. I do not get to keep this land no matter how much I worked it (unless I come into a vast amount of money!) and the second definition pretty well means any house in the suburbs is a homestead! So, what really is a homestead? What is homesteading?

The best way to answer this is to look at the general consensus. I have many friends who are what we would consider homesteaders. A homestead is a place where one tries to become more self-sufficient. I wonder why that is not in the dictionary. Even that is still rather vague. Can an apartment with a balcony of vegetables be considered a homestead? Can a house in the city with a few chickens and a garden be considered a homestead? Certainly a place in the country with a large garden, goats, chickens, sheep, and cows is considered a homestead, right? I suppose everyone would answer this question differently.

This is homesteading to me:

A homestead is a respite, a home with land to be able to succeed at becoming more self-sufficient. This place can be rented or owned. This place provides a basis for producing what one needs to live. So, homesteading is the verb here where one works to become less reliant on modern society and more secure in their own home as opposed to spending more time working outside the home and relying on utility providers, grocery stores, etc. for their needs. It is possible that this could take a lifetime. But it is worth the effort.

I often hear the argument that it is impossible to be self-sufficient. I suppose that depends on one's definition. Would you consider the Ingalls from "Little House on the Prairie" to be self-sufficient? I bet you would. They did go to the general store at times to pick up flour, cornmeal, sugar, a bit of candy, and some fabric. The question would be, if the store was not available, would they be alright? The answer would be yes. They would be alright, at least for a time. Would you consider the Amish self-reliant? I bet you would say yes. The home I visited of an Amish family last year was very simple. They had food stored in a makeshift root cellar (like mine), shelves of beautifully colored jars of produce (like mine), enough wood to get through winter (like us), and propane to light their house, run their stove, refrigerator, and a sewing machine. That is what threw me off! We use propane to help offset the heat and to run the refrigerator. It is very expensive and is getting quite nerve-rackingly low. Are we self-reliant? Not yet, in my book.

Why Is It So Important To Be Self-Reliant?

Why is it important? I mean, really, what is the big deal? A lot of folks are not really ready to give up their luxuries. Our bathroom was 35 degrees this morning. This is not for the faint of heart. My backside is still cold! But, it's important to me to become self-reliant for two reasons.

First of all, working for other people is too uncertain. We create our own business, our own crafts, our own classes, and yes we have to have faith that folks will buy or sign up, but we control our destiny and our mornings. The more we have to be away from the house working for someone else, the less we can do here, so the less self-reliant we are. We must make our living off of our homestead. Our living is a lot different than what it was ten years ago. To us a living was over $55,000 with a mortgage, car payments, utilities, food prices, gas prices, and all the other things we "needed". Now our living is around $24,000 if we want to be comfortable with wood, homegrown food, fish, and necessary items for our business, gas, rent, and animal feed. The first thing folks that want to homestead must realize is to be prepared to live on less. There is much to be done at the house. Canning, home business, chopping wood, year round growing of plants, animal care, but there is nothing sweeter than not worrying about where your next meal will come from and never sitting in a cubicle again.

The second reason it is so important to me to become self-reliant is because I need to be able to take care of my family, if necessary, in an emergency. This could be a wide spread power outage or blizzard, or worse. I would rather have a house full of necessities and not be wondering how I would get to the grocery store or if we were going to freeze to death. I do not know if folks realize the folly in relying on large companies for one's necessities. If it all came down to the wire, they don't give a hoot about your family and it would be quite wise to have a way to access water, heat, food, clothing, and protection.

Each year we do a homestead checklist and see what we need to do to become more self-reliant. Realize that I do not think those solar panels and their non-decomposing batteries, or wind power with its bird and bat killing capabilities are the answer. Living with less reliance on oil and gas is our goal.

Assess your goals. What do you need to do to become more self-reliant when it comes to heat, food, clothing, water, and protection?

- We have a wood cooktop/propane oven. A homesteader's dream? Yes. But, I do not want to rely on propane and the small wood compartment does not do much to heat this house. 44 degrees in the living room is just a bit too freaking cold for me. Our stove can be cooked on, heat a small portion of the house, could heat water if necessary, and is great. However, this year we will secure (somehow) a real wood cook stove that will sit in the living room that I can bake and cook on plus heat the rest of the house.

- Since we stopped eating meat I was able to clear out an entire freezer. The remaining refrigerator/freezer holds milk, fish, cheese, condiments, and vegetables. Is it possible to can fish? Should I can all the vegetables/fruits next year? How would we keep the milk cold? Particularly when milking starts again. I need an ice house. The back bedroom would seriously serve as a fridge right now, though. We really need that other wood stove!

- We have several wells on the property. We have a tiny bit of water saved in canning jars, but is there a way to access the wells without electricity? We are also incorporating a water harvest system this year.

- I have a hand washing unit for laundry and a great clothes line plus a huge drying rack for inside if it's stormy out. (We haven't used in a dryer in seven years.) We could live without the television and internet if we had too.

- I grew about a third of the items we preserved this year. I would like to grow sixty percent this year and plant several fruit and nut trees and berry bushes. I would also like to try my hand at growing mushrooms. I will incorporate container gardening, cold frames, and our garden plot to grow everything we love to eat. I would like to get a greenhouse as well. That would really boost our production.

- I am kicking myself, y'all, for selling my spinning wheel! I would like to get sheep and work on spinning again. I would like to learn to knit this year and make us some fabulous sweaters and socks. There is so much discarded fabric out there. I have tons myself. I would like to improve my sewing skills so that I can make more of our clothes.

- We would like to make the fences more secure this year so that we can let the animals graze on the ten acres. That would cut down on how much hay they need.

- I need to find a way to advertise and promote my classes so that we can pay for things like gas and car insurance, grains, animal feed, things like that.

- We will start cutting our own wood and collecting wood this year instead of paying so much to have cords delivered.

Well, I am sure there is more, but that is a good start and each year we get closer and closer to being self-reliant. Maybe that is the answer. Maybe self-sufficient and self-reliant are two different things. Either way, there is a great feeling of accomplishment and inner peace while performing simple tasks and caring for those you love on your own homestead.

Wishing you a prosperous and peaceful homestead this coming year!

8 Reasons You Need a Farmstead

1. You need less money to live. In our culture one of the most stressful parts of our day to day life is trying to find ways to make ends meet, to find ways to make more money. This is a vicious circle, because the more you make the more you spend.

Our journey may have begun way back when we took the Dave Ramsey courses at our church at the time. We cut up fourteen credit cards and have not looked back, nor do we hold a single one now. Our "emergency credit card" is cash stashed away for an emergency in the proverbial coffee can. If we don't have the money now to buy it, we won't have the money when the bill comes either! The course also showed us the follies behind borrowing and loaning. We never borrow money (from banks or relatives), and we don't loan out money. Gift or nothing.

All these principles helped us find our way to this homestead. We decided that the cushy job Doug held was not worth the money, since we spent it so quickly anyway. You will spend what you make. So, instead of making more money, we starting cutting bills. Expensive cable, gone. We'd rather be out in the garden watering, or chatting over a competitive game of Scrabble. The home phone became my cell phone. We do not have the fastest internet to Doug's dismay. We own really high mileage cars. We have relatively low bills so we need to make less money. This creates a sense of peace and a lot less fear and stress. This lifestyle requires less. One only needs a plot for a garden, a very good library book, and a cat.

2. You get to aide in creation. This is a pretty spectacular concept. You get to help God create a Garden of Eden right where you are. Your hands help create the beds of brilliant ruby tomatoes, the crisp lettuces, the sunflowers that help feed the birds. You get to grow plants that feed bees and butterflies. You get to create beauty all around you that will bring happiness to all that see it. It is a joyous privilege to be a creator.

3. You create positive living environments for animals. In a world of mass meat production, animals being shot up with hormones and drugs, ailing animals thrown into "dead" piles, and inhumane holding and slaughtering facilities, isn't it nice that you can do your small part

to help the animal kingdom? Whether you choose to eat your animals or not is irrelevant. For all their days they get to run in the sun, eat what they were intended to, be in contact with other animals, and receive much appreciated attention. Even if you only have four chickens, those chickens will lead a very good life and were lucky not to have fallen in the confines of a factory farm. It is a ripple effect, every bit of good adds up to much larger change.

4. Farmsteads diminish fear. In our packed cities, and even in the country, most folks rely on the water company to do their job. We assume that the water will always flow from the tap, the electric companies will always keep the electricity on so that the furnace will run, and the grocery stores will always be open. In a disaster (not talking zombie apocalypse here, more like tornados or floods) it is nice to know one could light the wood stove to heat the house, open water that has been stored, and go down to the farmstead grocery store, the root cellar, and bring up potatoes, jars of corn, and maybe some homemade wine. If a disaster strikes, Honey, you're gonna need it.

5. Human nature requires farmsteads. Cement sidewalks, air conditioned buildings, paved roads; our whole world is built to give the impression that we are controlling our environment. Our sensory is diminished, our creativity slows. A farmstead provides food for the senses. Smell the flowers, breathe in the fresh air, see the wide expanse of sky, touch the soil, and hear the buzzing of a honeybee. Being in nature also amplifies creativity and any number of brilliant ideas can come to you while walking through a garden, or a field, or watching a sunset. Creating your own farmstead (anywhere) allows your senses to be fed daily.

6. Farmsteads save the planet. Such a cliché anymore, Save the Planet! But whether you believe in climate change or not, whether you are sick of the fight between sustainable energy and homegrown oil, one thing cannot be denied; we are doing damage.

Just look down the block on trash day. Look around the shelves of department stores and big box stores, and grocery stores and see the boxes and packaging and cheaply made items from overseas that will be in the trash on trash day in a matter of months. It can be quite an eye opener if you see that all of that will end up in hidden landfills that we'd rather not think about. Think about the toxic chemicals (cleaning products) that we flush through our water. The pesticides that we add to the farms and gardens and lawns everywhere are slowly decreasing the bee population to a horrifying level.

We can do our part though. Grow organically on your own patch of earth, use your own homemade cleaning products, create your own ideal of reuse, recycle, and for heaven's sake, stop buying stuff! A farmstead inspires all of this. Houses are typically smaller for I'd rather be out hoeing than in the house cleaning. You can heat a smaller house easier and you certainly need less stuff. Homesteaders' packaging comes in reusable glass jars and there are many ways to reuse items on a homestead. (I am collecting the large cat litter containers to use as pots for the summer.) The beauty we create around us also reflects into the world and inspires us all to take care of our resources.

7. Farmsteads ensure health. In our battles to find good health, somewhere between doctors and fast food, in the gym, and with the psychiatrist, there is a place of perfect well-being. On a farmstead.

Mental health is ensured for it is impossible to be depressed or anxious sitting in a patch of corn. I assure you that roses do indeed medically perk up the brain and increase endorphins. To create something, to grow something, to fix something gives the mind such a sense of accomplishment, one we are missing in the common workplace. To feel important, needed, and accomplished keeps the mind happy and healthy. We cannot sit around all day and expect to be healthy.

Physical health is another part of the farmstead. Lift a couple of bales of hay, fix a fence, and hoe a new garden bed and you will cancel your gym membership right quick. Use the saved money to buy a new goat. Then you have fresh milk. The eggs from the chickens provide higher amounts of Lutein and Omega3. Less cholesterol and cortisol is found in farm fresh, humanely raised meat. And the organic vegetables from your plot have all their vitamins intact because they did not recently arrive from Peru. Fueling the body with amazing food and exercise outdoors is ideal for the human body. Growing your own medicine is empowering and takes away one's need to go to the doctor or pharmacist. (It also saves a whole lot of money that could be used for more hay.)

Spiritual health is every bit as important. A sense of overwhelming peace and hope can be found among butterflies landing on nearby lilies and hearing birds sing. It is difficult to be Atheist on a farmstead. To know that all our needs are supplied and to see the proof around you is incredibly powerful.

8. Farmsteads create community. The term "self sufficient" is really misleading. For we need people. I need Jill to barter with me so that I can have goats and then I need her to tell me when they are in labor. I need Sandy to grow some of the herbs I use in medicines for me. I need Lisa to show me how to knit. I need Rich to bring me trout. I need someone to grow organic grains for me. I need John to show us how to build a shelter for the animals (or just do it). I needed Deb to tell me to water more. I need Skip to tell me what our town has been like for the past seventy years. I need folks. Most of the time I like to be alone with my little world I've created over here but in a farmstead life, we need people. The benefits are tremendous. People stop and visit while we are out watering the gardens. We meet new friends. I am known as the herbalist with the pumpkin patch, a moniker I can be proud of. (I have been called worse.) A pumpkin patch makes folks smile. Bartering becomes the norm. Circles of familiar friends are discovered and life gets just that much sweeter.

So whether you are in town or in the country, have access to a balcony or a full acre, get going on that farmstead. You won't regret it.

Secrets to an Enchanted Life

1. Notice Something New in Nature Every Day.   This could be while walking down a city sidewalk to work or in your own field of hay. Take a moment to smell the air, see the different colors that nature has painted that moment, listen for birds, see butterflies flitting by, spy nests, and laugh at squirrels.

2. Do More of What Makes You Happy. I have a large coffee mug that I picked up in California with this saying on it. It pleases me and reminds me of a fundamental right; we can do what makes us happy. I spent too many years doing what I was "supposed" to do. Make people happy, do the proper thing, work hard, stay married (second times a charm), go to funerals, weddings, parties, events, stay friends with the same draining people. Slowly the creative, enchanted side of me started to leave. Stuck in the world of what I should do, left little room for what I wanted to do. Even though folks say you should do everything you have to do now and to do what you want later, I have noted too many times that later doesn't always come. No telling how long my lifespan is and I intend to do what I want now. If I am not incredibly close with the person I have no desire to go to funerals, or other hooplas. I will work for myself even if that means fewer luxuries. My luxury is my garden and baby goats and my warm bed at night.

3. Do Not Turn Down Opportunities or Invitations. Not the same thing as #2! At a market last Saturday a young woman asked quietly if I might like to come over for tea sometime. She lived in the trailer park across the street from where we used to live and was rather enchanted by my gardens. The hermit side of me would immediately dash such a notion. I am very busy! But, to meet someone new, to learn something new, to share your life for a moment with another spirit walking the same journey, one never knows what positive spin on one's life this could take. Invitations for wine and tea, walks, and new friends add glints of happiness and layers of memories upon our lives.

4. Adopt an Animal. Whether it is a kitten or a chicken, a dog or a goat, animals of all kinds add a certain pleasure to our lives that cannot be replicated with anything else. To run your fingers through a warm cat's fur, or laugh at a chicken running by with a worm, to

hug a crying baby goat who needs attention, or to take a tremendously happy dog on a walk, to stroke the neck of a beautiful steed, or hold a baby duckling in your hand. These are exhalation moments. Ones that bring the swirling world to a brief stop and time revolves around the animals that rely on you for care. My house may sometimes smell of cat boxes or worse, the dog may have gas, chicken poop may stick to our shoes, and there may be hay in my apron pockets, but I do not ever foresee Doug and I not having furry kids. They enhance our life far too much.

5. Do Not Worry About What Other Folks Think. Particularly family and friends. Sometimes peer pressure can be hurtful and cause worry. I do not care that we live in a little run down, cute house on rented property with all these animals. Years ago I had to stop caring what folks thought about us taking our kids out of the public school system and teaching them ourselves. They are intelligent, well educated, eloquent, grown children. I do not care what people say about our granddaughter not having vaccinations. She is the smartest child I have ever met. I do not care that my skirts are old and kind of ripped. That I am sensitive and get my feelings hurt easily. What happens when you decide this is your life and this is how you want it, or this is how it is, old friends and family back off and new friends and family step forward and your entire inner circle changes to like-minded people or just people that really love you for who you are.

6. Plant a Seed. A pot on the balcony will do. Or a large garden if you wish. But plant a seed or bring home an already planted strawberry plant or basil plant. Do something so that you can taste a bit of fresh food each day. Fresh food energizes the body and spirit and keeps us healthy and enthralled with unique flavors and textures. A garden or potted balcony is a lovely place to contemplate one's life and days. To be thankful and to enjoy a cup of coffee.

7. Pen a Letter. I write to my pen pals while Doug is shooting pool. In a darkened hundred year old building that has been a saloon for perhaps all of that time, I am surrounded by old ranchers and Vietnam vets who wonder out loud (and loudly), "What are you doing?" No matter how many times I tell them I am writing a letter, they reply, "No one writes letters anymore." How enjoyable to open

the mailbox to find a letter. A real one. Folded crisp paper, carefully scripted beginning turned illegible near the end as we try to write everything on our minds and happenings before our hand tires too much. Stamps and carefully addressed envelopes heading to destinations that I have not yet seen. Write to an old friend or aunt that would enjoy the antiquated pleasure of a letter.

8. Turn off the Television. For heaven's sake turn off the television! Do not use it as a babysitter. Do not let the kids play video games. Awake your husband. Get un-addicted from television shows. So much nonsense out there taking root in our psyches. If you need to relax, a drink and a book on the porch is lovely. A walk is even better. A walk with your spouse is time to talk and hold hands. A knitting project waits. So do homemade cookies. A spot in the garden with drawing paper. A telephone call to an old friend, or sister. Time is elusive. Invite the neighbor over for laughs. Be present.

9. Get Outside. Can you walk to work, or the mailbox? Can you get outside on your lunch hour? Can you sit outside and have lunch? Dinner? The outdoors is where our spirits can breathe. The stresses of life melt away. Enchantment begins. Watch a sunrise...or sunset. Smell a flower. Feel earth between your toes. Sit in the grass. Or just take a walk. Every moment outdoors fuels creativity and stress reduction. We were never meant to be cooped up indoors.

10. Notice and Memorize Moments. We had our annual party Saturday night. Rodney came over with the karaoke system. Tents and twinkly lights were erected and the cocktails and great potluck food were enjoyed to the sound of singing and the rodeo going on in the fairgrounds. Fireworks lit up the night later. Every time I am in a place with people, whether it is at my brother's wedding last week or at the party Saturday, I take a moment to look around, take it all in. Who knows how much longer I will have my grandparents, or more surprisingly, how long my friends may be here. Losing my dear friend, Nancy, so suddenly this last spring left a hole in my heart and I am now more apt to notice and enjoy the moment. The first annual party without her. I did not worry if everyone had a drink or a plate of food. Or if everyone was having fun or if I was being a good hostess. I just sat back and noticed people laughing, caught up with

everyone, appreciated everyone there. Gave hugs, sang, watched the sunset, and was thankful for all these good friends.

Enchantment and creativity are found all around us and in our hearts we want to be carefree. I hope you will find freedom and more glints of happiness and life moments with each passing day. See you on the porch!

How to Become a Homesteader (Finances)

Our homesteading school garners a lot of interest and folks of all walks of life are more and more interested in leaving the rat race and joining the simple life. Most people have a romanticized view of what homesteading looks like, but the good news is, most of those images are true. It is lovely to live so simply and to not worry as much and to have more freedom with time.

We have a lot of people ask how to get to this point. How do you achieve the homestead? How do you get your own place, your own farmstead? How do you leave your job? How do you walk away from your lifestyle?

Here is the very first thing that one has to realize, grasp, and accept before they pursue this lifestyle. You must be prepared to give up your way of life. You must be prepared to give up a lot of things, a lot of comforts, a lot, in order to get away with living this way. But you get much, much more in return.

1. Regarding Work: unless you are independently wealthy or are expecting an inheritance, you'll need to make an income. There are a lot of people with "regular" jobs looking to escape to this lifestyle but do not want to give up the RV payment, the car payment, the cable package, the electric run home, the big house, etc.. But, a lot of times the reason that people want to become homesteaders is to get away from those rat race jobs! To not be reliant on others to keep them employed. To not work 40+ hours a week breaking their backs and then expect to be able to go do chores and call in to work if a sick lamb is born. Homesteading is about being your own boss.

There are the few that enjoy homesteading on the weekends or love their corporate jobs. This is more about those of you that want to choose what you do from day to day, who want to live closer to nature, and who want to be less reliant on the system, and have faith in their abilities to provide for themselves.

There is a new wave of entrepreneurs coming up. People are realizing that four year college is not the answer most of the time for our young folk. Heading into their adult lives with debt is not a great way to start out. Trade schools are rising in popularity and for good reason. There are few people my age that know how to fix plumbing, who can do carpentry, or who can fix their own cars. We all got used to hiring people, and that is expensive. But if these young people can grab some of the training and jobs out there to do these things, they can work for themselves and make a fair income. Not just young people, if you need a new career, look into trade work. If you know how to do these things, focus your energies on those skills to make a homestead income.

I have friends that make their entire living off of farming. One needs less bills in order to achieve that. We make a very nice living (it may be considered poverty level, but it works for us!) teaching how to make herbal medicines, homesteading classes, and farming full time.

If you get your bills down low enough, an enjoyable part time job might be sufficient.

2. Bills: Do you need a cable package? Do you need television? Do you need internet? Can you use free Wi-Fi somewhere? Get your bills down as low as you can on paper and then you will see how much you need to make per month. Forget the five year plan, the "when we get this paid off" plan, "when we retire" plan. Life is short, life is waiting, act soon!

Take away preconceived notions. You do not need to own a lot of land to homestead. Find a cheap rental with a friendly landlord.

As you get involved in this lifestyle you will find that you will meet more and more likeminded people. Homesteaders are an amazing community of people that are always willing to help with advice and expertise and who love to barter!

3. Debt: It seems impossible to get rid of the debt we accumulated through student loans and losing our house from our previous lifestyle but we certainly aren't adding any more to it! We do not use credit cards. We do not take on debt. We highly recommend the Dave Ramsey program. Assume that if you can't afford it today, you can't afford it later! A cash based budget is easier to keep track of.

4. Rely on Yourself: Learn how to make alternative medicines. They are every bit as effective as pharmaceuticals. Barter for what you need if possible. Preserve as much food as possible. Heat your home with wood if possible. Make a list of where your money goes....doctors, grocery stores, clothing stores, etc., and see what you can do for yourself. Break it down even further. Crackers on your grocery list? Learn to make them!

It is empowering and takes some stress off of you if you can do it yourself.

5. Learn New Skills: Can you get a book on how to make home repairs? Can you learn to build a fence? Can you learn to make antibiotics? Can you learn to can? Yes you can! This is the first step in successfully becoming a homesteader and leaving the status quo behind.

We get to babysit our granddaughter while our daughter is at work part time because we make our own schedules. We have so much fun with that little munchkin. We have time to run around with our animals and enjoy the views here. We have few worries here. We are in control of our life and is there anything sweeter than that?

How to Become a Homesteader (Skills)

We try to learn two new skills each year. There are some skills that are imperative to the survival of a homesteader. Actually, not just for homesteaders, anyone who is trying to live as simply and on as few funds as possibly (less work for a paycheck equals more freedom to live life how you want). It is nice to have more than one person living on a homestead (doesn't have to be a spouse) because generally what one person can't do, or doesn't care to do, the other can. And for the things that neither are very good at, bartering with someone that has that skill set is invaluable. Here is a rough list of important skills to learn to be a homesteader.

1. Cooking: I have been cooking since I was quite small and Doug was a bachelor for some time before we got married so we both know how to cook. That doesn't mean that restaurants weren't our worst vice! We haven't sworn off restaurants completely and we do go out more than our other homesteading friends. I do, however, cook the vast majority of our meals. If I am too tired to cook in the morning Doug will fry up a delicious hash (fried potatoes, onions, garlic, eggs, and any vegetables or fish we have).

Cooking is not only important to the modest budget required in a homestead, but it is better for you as well. You need to stay strong while doing farm chores! It is also much more ecologically friendly. You can decide how many pesticides to put in your body, how many miles your food traveled, and how many boxes you put in the landfill.

We rarely buy anything in a box. We use whole ingredients and in bulk if possible. Grains, fresh vegetables fruits, the food we preserved, fish, legumes, eggs, milk, and cheese, make up our various meals along with a lot of great spices and flavor. It is easy to put together meals with so much selection. And because they weren't in boxes, but rather larger bags, they were cheaper too. I can add my own flavorings without all the additives.

2. Gardening: Being able to grow your own food is a wondrous thing. The cost of seeds is much less than the cost of groceries with the added benefit of being in the sunshine, knowing where your food came from, having all the nutrients still available, and helping out the bees. One can successfully garden in a plot, the front yard, in five

gallon buckets on the porch, anywhere really! I combine all of these to get enough space!

3. Canning: After World War II women wanted a different life. Canning, cleaning, country living, many normal ways of life were shunned in favor of city living, jobs, packaged food, and cleaning ladies. The typical pre-war lifestyle was thought of as mundane and peasant, if you will.

Canning is a great way to survive on a fixed income. By putting up all the produce the summer brings (even if that means buying a bushel from a nearby farm) we don't let all that glorious produce go to waste and come winter we scarcely ever need to go to the grocery store! Just look in the pantry!

Canning is enjoyable as well. It is a great sound when those jars click shut. It is particularly fun with margaritas and other women to help!

4. Fencing: This was one of the first things Doug had to learn and quick. Come two squirrely, runaway goat kids, we had to learn to reinforce and put up good fencing on the cheap. We have found that T-posts and pasture fencing are affordable options and moveable if necessary. We will easily be able to fence in a large area off of the current goat pen for the goats and new arrivals.

5. Building and Fixing: I grew up in a home where my mom taught us girls how to do every domestic chore. I am grateful for that. I have never pushed a lawn mower or changed my own oil though. My dad built their house by hand. He can fix anything, my brother can too, but I was not taught these things. Doug grew up in a house where if something broke, they called someone in. So, when we first started dating and something would break, I'd say, "Aren't you going to fix that?" and he would look at me like I was crazy. We spent a lot of money on hiring people over the years and we needed to learn how to build and fix things. This is a skill we will work on more this year. This is one that we barter classes or computer support for. I traded a class for a fabulous cold frame. We would like a better milking shed too. Neither of us even knows where to start! That is where knowing how to barter comes in handy. But we also need to learn for ourselves.

6. Animal Care: Animals are an important part of a homestead. For many they are a source of meat, but for this vegetarian farm, they are a source of food, fiber, and comedy shows. We love our chickens and their eggs. We love our goats, their milk, and the dairy products that we make from the milk. We can sell their kids and milk shares to help cover costs of feed. We are looking forward to our new sheep and their fleece as well.

We have needed to learn how to trim their feet, and how to know when they are sick, and what to give them. How to put an animal out of its misery (still working on that one, we are getting a revolver this year), and how to house and feed them. In my opinion, animals make the homestead. Sharing your life with other creatures makes things more complete.

7. Fire starting: We heat our house with wood and a propane heater. We got the bill for the propane. Next month we are putting in another wood stove that our friend found us so no more propane! We have a lot of wood stacked up and Doug learned to wield an axe. It keeps him in shape, helps him blow off steam, and keeps us in wood. But it took us a bit to figure out how to get the fire started easily! We weren't Scouts and we never needed to do much else but throw one of those ready to burn logs into an outdoor fireplace at a party. We learned quickly!

8. Sewing: Being able to mend old clothes or turn too old of clothes into quilts and projects saves you from having to purchase new items at the store. Remember, anything we currently purchase at the store we want to learn to do ourselves! I can make our granddaughter dresses, sew a semi-decent quilt, and mend, but I would like to learn this year how to sew more elaborate clothing, like men's shirts and dresses for myself.

9. Fiber Arts: Being able to knit a pair of warm socks is high on the list of skills I would like to master this year, along with animal shearing, carding, spinning, and dying yarn.

10. Learning to Entertain Oneself: Being able to not be bored easily and to be able to rest and entertain oneself is high in importance. We can't very well run off to see a stage production downtown anymore or away for a week in New Mexico. We also

don't have a big cable package or media entertainment. We read, write, draw, walk, have folks over, visit others, play with the baby, and sit outside in the sun.

Being a homesteader doesn't mean that one does less work. Nay, you might end up doing doubled! All of these skills take time. Time is what you will have and it is much nicer to be doing what you would like on your own time and schedule wherever you please. It is all good, pleasant work. And learning to rest and play is important as well. This is a great lifestyle. I highly recommend it if you are thinking of living this way! A good skill set makes it all the easier.

How to Become a Homesteader (Old Fashioned Items)

There was good reason for many of the items that we now view as quaint or wonder what they were for in antique shops. There are some items that will make your life much easier in your homestead. Some new, some not so new.

1. Oil Lamps: Oil lamps are functional and beautiful. In our effort to dramatically decrease our electricity use, we enjoy reading by these light sources. We have one large one on each end table and Doug bought me two that hang on the wall, one either side of our pillows. We have one on each table in the house and a few smaller ones that can be moved about. Lamp oil is fairly inexpensive and the lights give a soft glow to the homestead.

There was one evening when the electricity went out in the entire neighborhood at our last house. Doug and I did not even know until we got up and realized how dark it was outside! We just kept on reading.

The softer light also signals the body that it is time to settle down. Bright lights, LED lights, and blinking lights all act as stimulants for the body. It's no wonder there are so many sleeping issues out there!

You can pick up oil lamps at many big box stores, at thrift stores, or at Lehmans.com

2. Aprons: I may have about thirty-two of them but I am always on the hunt for more and love receiving them as gifts. I also make them but it is more fun to wear one that a nice great-grandma would have worn at one time. It honors those that came before us to wear something used with love.

The reason for aprons was simple. The ladies had only a few dresses and rather than mess them up every day and have ever more laundry (some chores never change) they wore an apron over the dress. This kept the dress clean and it was easier to wash an apron than a long dress. I wear my aprons out. I wear them cooking, cleaning, doing farm chores, gardening, at farmer's markets, and sometimes just out. I like to keep a tissue, a bit of cash, my phone, and a pocket knife in the pocket. I don't have to lug around the suitcase of a purse I have!

3. Pocket Knife: Doug and I got each other lovely turquoise knives. But a good old fashioned Swiss would do nicely as well. I have walked around with a steak knife in my pocket before getting a pocket knife. A pocket knife folds up, y'all. Just get one. You can easily cut fresh greens, snip the twine off a bale of hay, or any number of things that come up. Cut open an apple, get one with a wine cork on it... instant picnic! But really, yesterday I went to feed the goats forgetting that it was a new bale and pulling and pushing around the hay bale doesn't get it undone. I forgot my knife in the house. Back in my apron pocket it went.

4. Work Gloves: It took us awhile but it wasn't long before we figured out that we needed some work gloves. We had several lying around but we keep them by the door now. From mending fences, to digging fresh soil, from picking up a sick chicken, to bringing in firewood, gloves are imperative.

5. Cast Iron Pans: I spent a good many years buying those cheap Teflon pans in lovely colors only to get Teflon in my eggs and needing new pans. We have a nice collection of cast iron now (always on the lookout for a new piece) and they will be passed down to our children's children's children! They stay in great shape, can be whipped into shape if they have been neglected too long, can go from fire to stovetop, and are great for cooking.

6. Cuckoo Clocks and Wind up Clocks: Same reason as the oil lamps, should the power go out you wouldn't even know! We keep our clocks wound and love the gentle ticking. The bird that appears thrills our granddaughter and visiting children (and many adults). We don't have any clocks with that dreadful LED light up display. The last one was discretely placed in the giveaway pile. I like the feel of a vacation home. I like that I live in a vacation home. Plenty of things to read and do, not a lot of electric stimulation, just gentle lighting and sounds.

There are many nice things to have on a homestead; seeds, tools, books, board games, matches, coffee, a man... but these six things will get you started!

.

How to Become a Homesteader (Thrift, Barter, Splurge)

Finding balance is one of the things we all strive for in every aspect of our lives. Becoming a homesteader is about living the life you want, that you dream of. It's about taking chances and knowing you can live on less. It is about spending time in the gardens and with animals and friends and not giving our life to a corporation, who will have you replaced by the time you hit the parking lot, or grave. This is about relationships; with community, with friends and family, with nature, with God. This is about freedom. When we are living on less, we need to know when to be thrifty, when to barter, and when to splurge.

Being thrifty means that we reuse a lot of things and we don't produce a lot of waste. This is helpful on our pocketbooks and the earth. We find we need less. We don't go to an office job so we don't need really nice clothes, nor do we worry too much about our appearance. We use our clothes until they are torn. Our cars have to be practically falling apart while driving before we get a "new" one. We read books from the library and rarely purchase new. We reuse rubber bands to fasten stems of greens together to sell. We save all of our twist ties and use them to stake plants to trellises and tomato cages. Wine corks can be put in the bottom of pots before filling with soil for drainage. Boxes that are too small to put in the garden or use to store canning jars get torn up and are used as fire starters. Wine bottles get turned into oil lamps. The wicks can be bought at Lehmans.com or at some wine stores. Just add lamp oil!

Bartering is imperative in the homesteading world. Being able to trade for services that we cannot do ourselves helps us to live on a small income and helps connect us to others. Rod put up a screen door for us and Doug cleaned up his computer. We are trading one of Elsa's kids for one of Jenet's Nubian kids. Last year Joan and I traded canned goods so we would have a bit of variety. We barter herbal medicines for a lot of things!

When to splurge? Buy good quality feed for your animals. Buy organics for yourself if you didn't produce them. When buying tools, buy the best you can so you don't have to repurchase. Buy quality seeds. Not everything need be cheap. Sometimes a bargain costs much more in the end.

Then there are other types of splurges. We live this way to enjoy life. I was getting darn sick of boxed wine! If it's under $15, a bottle is worth it. One can find a great deal of fabulous wines in that price range. And if Doug and I aren't running around wine bars all week like we used to, you can bet your overalls that I am going to enjoy my glass of single vineyard, estate grown wine with dinner!

This weekend we are taking Emily, Bret, and our sweet Maryjane Rose up to Boulder to celebrate Emily's birthday a bit early. I bartered for the rooms at a gorgeous Bed and Breakfast. We will splurge on great meals and make fond memories with our children.

Enjoy the good life today folks. Life is sweet.

How to Become a Homesteader (Community)

In this "How to Become a Homesteader" series we have talked about leaving the rat race for greener pastures, eliminating a lot of unnecessary bills and cutting others. We have lowered our need for so much income and found a good trade or homestead job that we can bring in what little we do need. We have discussed farm animals and heating with wood and telling time on a cuckoo clock. We have figured what skills we ought to pick up and now we are ready to roll. But there is one very important aspect to becoming a homesteader. Community. It seems that would be opposite to what we are trying to achieve. We want to be self-reliant, grow our own food, take care of ourselves, and have less fear. But, what we are really doing is becoming less reliant on big corporations and more reliant on ourselves and each other. That is how we were made.

When you become a homesteader you will naturally attract and meet other homesteaders. Each has something to offer. It is one big circle out here. A gentleman took my herbalist class who has a tree service who got us our first cords of wood and will provide me with wood chips. He is teaching me more and more about wild plants. I make herbal medicines and Doug fixes computers but we need some help learning how to build things and with cars. We have found more and more people that need what we have and can offer what we need.

There is comfort in being near close friends and family and a need to be near others. The old saying still rings true, "Many hands make light work." And since each of us has our own gifts and talents, we can come together to provide a completely self-reliant community.

Part 2 (Farming, Providing Your Own Grocery Store)

5 Steps to Starting a Farm

So you have decided to start a farm. You have a burning desire that is unquenchable, filled with seed catalogues and pioneer books. You have a desire to grow your own food. You are fed up with what the government deems safe for consumption. You have decided to take matters in your own hands and will feed your family yourself. Organic, heirloom, homegrown, beautiful produce will fill your yard, and your pantry will become your grocery store.

Perhaps you also desire to feed others, share the bounty of healthy vegetables. Maybe you want to start a community garden, or teach people to farm. You love making $1.25 an hour, working for eighteen hours a day in the summer and autumn and enjoy dirt, bugs, and cold beers after weeding. You are in good company, my friend, make yourself at home. Now let's talk about how you make this a business.

1. Find out the rules in your area. Some of you may not even be able to have a clothesline let alone a farm. It does not matter how much land you have or what your soil type is. You can fix all that. You can use containers, raised beds, and the side yard. You can amend the soil with compost. On our last farm we were on two-thirds of an acre. Essentially two lots in town. Because we lived in a small town, no one had thought to make a ton of rules yet. I asked the town administrator and was given the go for farm animals as long as I don't get carried away (whoops) and the neighbors don't complain. Simple enough. I can farm to my heart's content. We rent, but the landlord is out of the state and as long as our rent comes in regularly, they don't care what we do.

I planned grand schemes of pumpkin festivals, a roadside stand, and folks coming over to pick up their vegetables. That is where I ran into trouble. I am zoned residential, not commercial. I can grow and sell everything somewhere else, but not on my own property. No businesses allowed. Deal with what you have but in the next place, check ordinances!

On our new farm, we are zoned agricultural and are in an unincorporated area. Now with the landlord's blessing, we can have those festivals.

2. Choose a name and make a logo. We did a contest on our Facebook page and a gentleman picked the perfect name for us. Our family has always loved autumn and attends pumpkin festivals. The movie, "The Legend of Sleepy Hollow" is memorized and quoted throughout the year. We even have a cat named Ichabod Crane. We love the colors of fall and especially pumpkins. So when Pumpkin Hollow Farm came up as a suggestion, we grabbed it! Doug said that we don't live in a hollow though. No imagination, I tell you. I showed him where the ground was slightly lower in front. Done. We are on a Hollow.

Now Google your name. Make sure there aren't two million entries for Old McDonald Farm, or whatever you come up with. There are a few Pumpkin Hollow Farms but they are in other states. We then checked to see if the domain name was available (more on that in a few) and if the Facebook page was available. Pumpkin Hollow Farm was born.

Draw a logo or have someone do it for you. For our Garden Fairy Apothecary logo I chose a beautiful and eye catching fairy from free stock photos. The problem was that I cannot blow it up for larger advertising (It was a GIF, to make it sparkle). My art banner has one of my paintings portrayed on it. When we took the photo of the painting, it was easily blown up to make a stellar banner. I painted an Americana style pumpkin and that will become our logo on the banner this year. HalfPriceBanners.com or your local office supply store can make banners for you.

3. Register your name. The Secretary of State website for your state is your next stop. For roughly $25 you claim your name. Now, all hell could break loose and you could decide against having a farm. That is fine; registering your name doesn't make you have to have a farm. It just makes sure that no one else takes your name within the state.

4. Market your farm goods. If you can set up a roadside stand, do it! If not, then you may want to check into farmer's markets in your area. Google "Farmer's markets in_____ (enter your town name)" and you will find the markets near you. There should be a link to their website or at the very least their contact information. Lately I have been able to reach prospective markets by finding them on Facebook.

You will need to fill out an application. There is often a fee to get in ranging from $5 to $200. There will be market fees each week ranging from 10% of your sales to $100 a week base. Choose your markets wisely. Just because they are more expensive does not mean they are a better market.

Be prepared for a lot of hard work. Folks stroll down the lanes at farmer's markets and see the people running the booths and mistakenly think that this is easy. Be ready to get up before dawn, harvest, finish packing the car, have your lunch ready (and breakfast, and coffee, and snacks) and after taking care of the animals, stumble over to the car. If you don't get there early someone will take your spot. It is rather competitive at the markets. Just smile and get there early. Once everyone is set up the ugliness goes away and everyone is friendly again.

Farmer's markets aren't always the best way to make money because the market managers want their share too and folks that visit the market seem to think it is a swap meet. Pick your prices, be proud of your work, and stick to your guns. Display is everything. Do not make people come into the booth to see your wares. They will not venture past the imaginary line in the front of the tent. I promise you. Set the table up close to the front of the tent. Use bright colors and unique display pieces to show off your items. Have a banner made so folks know who you are. It is best to sign up for markets in February. They fill up.

Also look into local festivals. Most towns have a celebration that has vendors. That is a great way to meet local people and let them know what you are doing. There are also co-ops or you can sell from the front yard if the town will let you.

5. Advertise the farm. Make fliers and put them around town and on community boards.

Get a website. Go Daddy is a good place to register your domain. They have great templates that make it very easy to set up and design a website. You just fill in the text and upload pictures. The rest is designed for you. For $10 a month, it is worth it!

Start a blog or write articles for local papers.

We made brochures this year and handed them out at the market, put them in packages we shipped, and have them on community boards. This has really increased interest.

6. Find out if the areas that you are going to be selling in charge taxes on food. A lot do not, some do. If you need a tax license then you can go to your local tax office and apply for a number. Send your sales tax in quarterly. For income tax, fill out a Schedule F. Here you claim your income but also write off chicken feed, seeds, and beer! Well, maybe not beer.

7. Order seeds. You probably already have some. Keep in mind that organic and heirloom seeds keep history and health alive. At the very least, farm sustainably. I love Seed Savers, and other heirloom companies. If you are ordering corn, order organic seeds!

8. Don't limit yourself to produce. You can sell a table full of carrots and only go home with sixty bucks. Think eggs, canned goods, meat, vanilla extract, baked goods, or homemade vinegars. Anything else that you do or make, consider adding it to your list of goods. We would not be able to survive as farmers alone. Variety is the key. A bit of this, a bit of that. I also promote my classes as our school is what pays the bills.

Now that you have done all that, you are ready to call yourself a farmer. So, like the rest of us, you must wait patiently until spring. Happy Farming!

Farming Lessons (Turn on the Water!)

It was a beautiful morning yesterday. The calm before the storm. The chickens at Debbie's house were playing. Her chocolate lab waited patiently for us outside the garden gate. All was well in the greenhouse for my "farming without killing plants" lesson.

In the outside beds we planted rows of carrots, cauliflower, and kale. The kale we planted a month ago never came up probably due to our fanatical weather and the extreme cold temperatures. This time should work! It's May 1st for crying out loud!

Then I helped her prepare a bed for planting. A lesson like no other. She sprayed it down very well, puddles welled up, and the soil was lovely and damp. We turned the soil with a spade. Dry. The ground was dry! I sprayed it really well for a second time. Turned it with the spade. Dry. Debbie mentioned that this scenario is the very reason many gardens to do not succeed. We sprayed it once again and it still was not damp through and through. The fourth time did the trick. My lesson? Never assume that because the top layer is wet that anything below is drinking water! Always use a water gage or the poor (wo)man's water gauge... your finger. The soil should be damp up to the second knuckle, if not, it needs water! I came straight home and turned the sprinklers on!

This is a long time idea in my head that I have to reverse. Reading gardening magazines and books for 20+ years has taught me one thing....don't over water! It causes diseases, fungal stuff, root rot and possibly world hunger. I have adhered to that sentiment with fervency. Don't over water! Here is the one thing they never specified. They aren't talking about Colorado or other dry areas. It's so dry here your nose may start bleeding at a moment's notice, so dry weeds died last year here! One would really have to work at it to over water in a dry state like this. I have been more diligent, twice daily checks on the soil in the garden. The reason I have NEVER had a carrot germinate is because the soil must remain moist the entire time until it gets its foothold. So, my soil has been consistently wet. It will need more once the roots spread down and need more drinks. The radishes have germinated in thanks.

In my garden, there are onions and garlic coming up, the herbs have returned, last year's onions that never came up are making a grand display in the wrong bed, and the cold crop seeds are slumbering quietly just beneath the surface which I hope by this weekend will be light carpets of tiny greens.

Debbie's herbs are so happy in her greenhouse they were jumping ship. Comfortably spreading out and lounging all over the bed. Because a good chunk of them needed to be evicted, I was the proud new recipient of twelve pots of oregano and cilantro. Which brings me to a great way to spread the wealth among farmers. Wendy brought me a few chive plants she split off, Diane is bringing me borage. Don't worry about having herbs that spread all over, split them up, stick them in a pot and give as instant gifts!

Early Crops for Spring (and planning the whole season)

"Take me home, country roads, to the place...I belooongg!" I was belting out my favorite John Denver song while tilling the sweet ground. The few inches of leaves (from my neighbor's trash last fall) and compost that I put on before the fierce winter weather did the ground good. It is dark and fragrant. The moisture stayed in many parts of it. This winter has been the most moisture we have received here in a long time and though I am still cold, it is nice to have so much damp ground. The pastures last year were so dry that hay spiked in price, animals went hungry, people panicked. The air is sweet with cool snow.

I raked back the majority of the unbroken-down mulch to the side. I gently tufted the soil with a rake, not turning it (too many nice microorganisms workin' for a livin' down there!), just loosening the top. Mulch will return once the plants are up.

I made an impromptu chart on the back of an index card during a sudden moment of gardening inspiration in January. I listed all the seeds to be planted in April (my early crops), all the ones that are planted third week of May (summer crops), and the ones that will be replanted the end of July and August (late crops....same as the early crops). I have eleven raised beds so I had to do some fancy finagling to get everything to fit. So I gave each bed a number and set to work jotting down what should be planted where. What will have time to finish growing in order to put in summer crops? Where will I have space to put in late crops and still have room for perennials and medicinal herbs?

Collard greens, Swiss chard, two kinds of kale, radishes, and two kinds of lettuce went into bed 1 which will be followed by tomatoes and peppers with greens continuously grown around them.

In a brief moment of gardening brilliance I set up three tomato cages and planted peas around the perimeter in a circle in lieu of a trellis. The peas and a few red potatoes and the most beautiful scarlet carrots went into bed 3 to be followed by soybeans and lettuce.

The limited potatoes are because I purchased them from the nursery then left them on the car floor, where they were then trampled by various teenagers' feet and piles of this and that. The remaining potatoes are shriveling and look rather pathetic but I still intend to plant them today in the potato barrels.

Cabbage and cauliflower went into bed 4 nestled in with surprise onion shoots from last year. I don't have the heart to pull them out. I will be lucky if the delicious cabbage and cauliflower ever transpire, we have a short growing season and bugs love them so I don't have anything planned for bed 4. Just a nice, long luxurious growing season for the cruciferous delicacies I love.

The garlic is coming up with frost burned tips, slow but sure. I do hope they make it! One cannot survive in the kitchen without a smidge of garlic.

Onions went in to bed 8. The possibly dead...possibly sleeping... Cabernet Sauvignon grape vine slumbers (hopefully) next to them. And in a fit of ridiculous hopefulness, Brussels sprout seeds joined the onions in bed.

The snow gently covered them for the last two days since I planted. Today should shine bright and cool. We will be nearing temperatures in the 70's by the weekend and early germinated shoots ought to be sticking their heads up to peek at their new world. I will have my face to the sun singing, "Take me home, country roads....."

Creating a Beautiful Tea Garden

Creating a beautiful tea garden this year will not only bring great happiness, but also provide free medicine in the garden, help feed the bees and butterflies, and can be grown anywhere from an apartment balcony to a forty acre parcel.

Herbs don't require a lot of water once they are established so they can survive droughts, but they do appreciate a light watering daily if it is available. Herbs are easy to grow and affordable. I often have trouble starting herbs from seed outdoors. Too many factors, birds, wind, and I don't have the room indoors but for $3 or less I can go to my local nursery and pick up one pack of my desired herb and it will spread and thrive throughout the summer. Friends and fellow gardeners are also good sources for a small divide of herbs. If you do not want them to take off like wild fire then plant them in pots, whether on the porch, or in the ground to help keep them from flitting about. Then mulch with wood chips or straw. At the end of the season give them some compost and cover with straw for the winter. Some Mediterranean herbs, such as Lavender and Rosemary, will be annual in mid to northern climates, but can easily be replaced or overwintered in the house.

When starting, place a large flattened cardboard box, several layers of newspaper, or straw to desired space. This is best to let rest for up to six months. Dig into the soil just where you want to plant and add a bit of compost and garden soil and mix well. One can create fantastic designs, circular walkways, or checkerboards, or simple lines. Herbs can also be added in with vegetables as they act as beneficial partners. Bugs that love to eat plants are not attracted to herbs and may bypass the whole tomato patch if they only see the basil!

My choices for a tea garden are:

Chamomile- any variety- Dainty, beautiful, used as a calmative, sleep aid, heartburn relief, digestive distress, mild pain reliever.

Mints: peppermint, spearmint, chocolate- Hearty, fragrant, used for digestive distress of any sort, fever reducer.

Basil (any variety) - May act as annual in many climates, used for digestive distress and to fight colds and viruses.

Motherwort - Watch out for stickers! Used to moderate hormones, heart support, and fights colds.

Monarda - also known as Bee Balm- Used to fight viruses and assist with memory.

Purple Coneflower - also known as Echinacea- Used as anti-biotic, cancer fighter, and immunity support. Use topically on wounds.

St. John's Wort - Used for anti-depressant and anti-anxiety medicine, helps heal nerve damage, strong pain reliever.

California Poppy - Easy to grow, used as a strong pain reliever.

Skullcap - Controls seizures, acts as strong pain reliever.

Roses (any variety) - Mild pain reliever, mild anti-depressant. Rose hips can be made into tea for arthritis pain. Highest fruit in Vitamin C.

Yarrow - white variety- Used internally for heart and vein support. Externally crush flowers and apply to wound to stop bleeding.

Use leaves and flowers in any blend you desire for flavor or benefit. To dry for winter, cut herbs and place in a paper bag clearly marked with contents. Three weeks later the herbs will be dried and can be placed in a canning jar.

To the garden add a table and chairs, a bird bath, and bring a cup of tea out to your tea garden to relax and enjoy.

What to Do With All That Poo

As Doug and I were shoveling alpaca poop onto the garden beds yesterday I said lightly, "You sure can't be bothered by poop if you live on a farm, can you?!" He laughed and agreed and we continued shoveling. I did not know that I would be around it so much post baby diapers. But there it is, now what to do with it?

The nice thing about alpaca and goat droppings is that it won't burn plants. It adds nitrogen to the soil but does not have to be composted. It can be added directly around plants and into garden beds. From poop pile to garden bed. Instant fertilizer. If you know someone that has animals, they will likely share. It is an added benefit to adopting alpacas or goats, no more Miracle Grow!

The chicken coop is full of future nutrition for the soil but it needs a bit more time. Believe me, six months on a farm goes real fast though. I have a compost bin that Doug easily made out of discarded pallets. In the first one, the pile starts. Coffee grounds from the coffee shop and the kitchen, tea bags, and other items I wouldn't put in the chicken food go in the pile along with the soiled chicken bedding.

When Nancy and I saw Joel Salatin two summers ago he mentioned that leaving the bedding in the coop all winter and just adding more as needed creates a warm space for the animals. In the spring, we are to shovel out the foot high plus pile of bedding and move it to the compost pile. Nancy didn't like this idea when she tried it. She has a lot more chickens than I do and for her the smell was overwhelming. The floor of my coop is dirt and it works well for me. Next month I will scoop out the soiled bedding and leftover scraps they didn't want (orange peels and such) and throw them in the first open bin of compost. He also mentioned that using straw is what creates the ammonia smell. I stopped using it and started using the pine shavings he suggested. The coop does not smell bad at all. However, now I learn that ducks will eat pine shavings so we will be back using straw soon. So, in this case, I may clean out the coop four times a year instead of two.

Scooped into the wheel barrel and thrown into its requisite side, it will be topped with some dirt or finished compost and left to complete. (Note: I constantly forget to turn my compost. It never looks completely black and finished, but it still works.) In the fall when I go to add compost to the cleaned out beds, it will be perfect. Then the bedding from the summer coop pile will be cooking away in the second open area of the compost bin and will be ready to apply in spring.

The goat poo is new to us this year. It will not easily be picked up in their pasture as they drop small and many pellets. I'd be raking for a week. However, their bedding will get changed out next month from their igloo and that will go into the cooking pile of compost.

Dog and cat feces may not go into the pile. It will decompose in the grass, true, but just like ours, one would need a composting toilet and high heat to kill the bacteria present. Doug and I are planning on getting a composting toilet in the next house though!

Human urine kick starts the whole process. However, raised in a home of decorum and higher society than most folks I know, Doug refuses to pee on the compost pile. (Of course we are open to a major thoroughfare and close neighbors.)

I used to think the chickens were going to give me too much compost to use. But I find myself in constant lack. The more I garden, the more I need. The larger this farm gets, the more I need. Even if one lived in a house smack dab in the middle of Denver one can use the compost from the allotted chickens and goats there. It goes faster than you think!

Manure tea can also be made with droppings and poured on house plants or outdoor beds. Just make sure the manure sat for six months if it isn't from an alpaca or goat.

I never thought in my life I would be writing about poop. It just goes to show, never say never and having a farm changes you.

Vegetables Playing Nice

We hear about companion planting often; combining plants together that are beneficial. Sometimes they flag down good bugs or bees for pollination, or sometimes they repel insects that enjoy eating their companion. They like each other. Basil and tomatoes. Potatoes and greens. Corn and squash. All good friends. I do companion plant but I do more than that. Even if I did have a zillion acres, I wouldn't mono-crop, meaning long rows of one plant. I know in commercial farming that it is considerably easier than digging out the cabbage from the lush onion tops, but I will probably never be that big! My real reason for growing plants all together in the same space is...well, space!

Now that we are trying to provide most of our own food and do some market growing, the corn cannot leisurely take up all that space. It best share. There is a full foot between the stalks. Squash and melon plants can be meandering around down there keeping weeds down. There is also room for some beans to climb up the corn stalk. (Sounds like a nursery rhyme!) This, of course, creates what is known as the Three Sisters, the Native American form of gardening. Yes, they are beneficial plants for each other but they also save on space.

Any blank few inches of dirt gets spinach, kale, chard, or lettuce seeds added to it. Baby greens are delicious, good for us, and easy to grow. They get put everywhere.

Onions share space with neighbors above ground, namely cauliflower, cabbage, and Brussels. Potatoes share with sunflowers. We have Irish blood in us, we need potatoes. When ours sprouted and ran for the hills in the root cellar, we were saddened. Thank goodness the ones at the store were available. This year we are planting them everywhere, in barrels, next to the extra row of beans, next to the carrots, and in another large raised bed.

The first set of lettuce and greens that I planted early were sparse and even though I can harvest them still, there is a lot more space in that bed. I could plant more greens or soybeans, or whatever I have left seed wise. Probably shouldn't plant pumpkins, they would pummel the little lettuce guys once they started spreading! Common sense helps with gardening. (I could use a smidge more...)

One can also think this way; something growing underground (potatoes, carrots, turnips...), something growing short that is early (lettuce, kale, collards...), and something that takes a while to get harvested (Brussels sprouts, cabbage, beans...), and make them share a bed. They all have enough room.

Now you never have to say your garden is much too small. You can have pots, five gallon buckets, trash cans, upside down tomato plants, and all the vegetables in the garden playing nice and sharing the soil. Just envision that harvest!

Trenches, Water, Mulch, Reseeding

I suppose a drip system would be the most effective way to adequately water without wasting and would save time. Doug and the neighbor laid out their respective plans over the winter for an elaborate drip system for our gardens. However, come spring we had enough budgeted for a new hose and maybe a sprayer. A drip system didn't fit into our meager farmstead funds!

The system we came up with wouldn't work in clay soil or in humid environments, but here in the high plains of arid Colorado, it works really well. It also saves us a lot of money on the water bill. I planted the seeds directly in trenches which were about six inches deep in some spots. We can water quickly by filling the trenches with a few inches of water which happens in ten seconds per area. It seeps in quickly and keeps two inches of soil wet for the next twenty four hours or so. The plants are protected from the wind and the moisture doesn't get whisked away so quickly.

In the garlic, onion, and potato rows I used the hoe to create small trenches along the sides of the rows. I can quickly fill them with an inch of water and they will seep in right to the roots.

Keep the soil covered! Open up a space in the wood chips, straw, newspaper, or whatever mulch you are using until you see the soil. Add a little compost and soil mixture if it is un-amended soil and plant seeds directly there. As the plants grow I leave a little space around the stems so they won't rot, but the entire area gets a nice blanket of weed squashing straw. This is a far easier way to keep up with the straggly and strangling crab grass and other fun weeds here. It really does slow down the weed growth and keeps the moisture in so that on some days we do not even have to water.

My biggest failures for the first twenty years of gardening came from these factors. Not enough water. Not enough weed control. And not enough diligence planting seeds. If seeds didn't come up, I felt like that particular bed was a failure. I had never heard of the saying, "Plant Three; one for God, one for the birds, one for me." Boy, is this true! Every third seed seems to come up. The birds take, no doubt, and apparently there is a tithe involved with planting. So, if some seeds don't come up, I am now out there planting another seed where I want it. All along the pumpkin patch there were spaces of missing plants. I just reseeded them. Same with the corn. Same with the brassicas. Through the middle of June one can keep planting summer crop seeds that will be ready for harvest and mid-July for fall crops.

These are three ways to assure good basic crops. Now we just hope for great weather and that Mother Nature looks kindly on our gardens!

Part 3 (Farm Animals)

How Much Does it Cost to Have a Farm Animal?

We knew how much it cost to buy the farm animals. Approximately two or three dollars per chick. $200 per alpaca (that was a smoking deal). $200 for the pair of adorable goats to be bartered for herbal medicine. (Another great deal. We should be able to sell goat babies for $200-$300 each!)

What we didn't know, and couldn't seem to get answers for, was how much is it to raise these guys? How much to feed them? Twenty dollars a month? Two hundred dollars a month? I needed to know if I would have to return the farm animals after three weeks if we couldn't afford it. I keep a good budget and I save up money for months in advance because our main income is earned during the summer. So, if some farm kid is going to eat us out of house and farm, Lord, I need to know about it!

I have gathered the numbers for all of you out there wanting to get a few cute farm animals yourself.

Alpacas are surprisingly affordable. The upfront cost can make you choke (count on $300 for a fiber boy up to $20,000 for a prized breeding girl) but once you get the little guys they don't cost much. We're talking one bale of hay between the both of them. Around $13 a month. With pine shavings and the pellets that have their minerals in it takes us to twenty. So, each fiber boy costs $10 a month. It's a good thing they don't cost much to feed because any animal that is that fluffy and cute should allow me to go snuggle with it. No can do. They don't come near me. Sad.

Goats eat a tad more, but not much. They love to eat. We got a pregnant mama here. They don't need the grain. (I was told at church yesterday by Jill. We spoil them a tad too much perhaps.) So with pine shavings, this makes the girls about the same. $10 a piece per month. We'll give some sweet feed in a few months when we are milking Katrina, so that will raise it up slightly. Jill gave us a good start on minerals. So, when we do have to purchase minerals and the sweet feed, we may be looking at $15 a piece per month. I have Nigerian Dwarves, so a larger breed would probably eat more.

The chickens....wouldn't you expect them to be the cheapest? They are giving us eggs to pay for their room and board. We feed organic feed. It's not that much more than the GMO stuff. They have been going through much more lately because of the cold and lack of forage (and lack of things to do, in my opinion). $36 dollar a month plus pine shavings which will take us to roughly $40 a month. At the two to three eggs a day from fifteen hens and their useless (but good looking) husband, that makes each dozen of eggs cost $6 a piece. No profit. But, we do have to consider that we don't buy eggs either. So, I am okay with that cost.

The greyhound costs $20 a month and eight cats cost $60 a month. So, in the end, the cats are the ones eating us out of house and farm. They better get back to mousing!

Of course these costs don't take into consideration veterinarian costs. But, we rarely use a vet. We are herbalists and teach people how to help their own animals. Not much we can't help take care of. So, that saves us a tremendous amount of money having that knowledge. One would need a vet to do surgery and for major emergencies, but just having a cat can place you at risk for having a huge vet bill in an emergency, so I don't count vet costs because that would come out of an emergency fund.

It is nice though, to see a general cost of feed and housing. A house is much more of a home with a rooster and a goat, don't you think? Now, how much does it cost to have a sheep?

Chickens

Dinosauresque bundles of fluff commonly kept for eggs and laughs.

Bringing Baby Home

In true mothering fashion, I worried. We bought a red light to warm them. Our friends who were moving lent us their little chicken feeder. We used a little china saucer for water (couldn't think of anything else...these are fancy girls!). We found a plastic storage tub and lid. We went to work. We set up the plastic tub in the chicken coop. We put pine shavings in it and the little chicken feeder with chick starter in it. We chose organic. We did not feel we needed medicated, genetically modified feed in our chickens any more than in our children! We put a little bowl of chick grit in there to help the little floofies process their food. The water went in and the light hung over one side of the box, very close to the top. The lid would cover the rest of the box and towels would be on top to cover drafty openings. Don't want the darlings to get chilled.

Then we went to get the little ones. Andy was home from college and went with me to the feed store to pick up our chickens that we had chosen. I had waited too long to reserve the breeds I had read about so I had to choose from what was left. Instead of Buff Orpingtons I got Golden Buffs (who are wonderful layers and very sweet). There were two little California white girls there that I thought were adorable in a cage unclaimed. In the box they went. The two black girls were irresistible. Jersey Giants; I couldn't wait to see how big! In they went with the other girls. We were on our way home with a cardboard box of chirping cuties.

In the coop, we took each baby out and dipped her little beak into the water so she would start drinking. They immediately took to it to my great relief. We placed them one by one in the box after their drink and several kisses. One of the wonderful things about baby animals is how they can make tough men melt. Seeing a nineteen year old young man kissing and cooing at baby chicks was heartwarming and I wished that I had raised the kids out here with farm animals. But better late than never, I guess! The kids kept disappearing to the coop. If Shyanne were depressed we could find her out talking to the chickens. Emily didn't stay away for long and each girl had named one of the chickens and deemed her their own. Friends came over to see the petite chirpers and much joy was spread from ten little chickens.

We learned that we should raise the light up a few inches each week for eight weeks. If they were cold, they would huddle under the light and I knew to lower it a bit. If they fled to the outer reaches of the box, they were too hot and I could raise it a little. But most of the time, it was just right. The girls thrived.

The reason we took extra chickens home is because a few people bit their lip, sighed, or otherwise gently let us know that we should take more than six home as we are certain to lose a few. For no apparent reason than what I deemed "Sudden Chickie Death Syndrome" one of the buffs was dead. We mourned and took her out of the box. Laverne and Shirley, the black Jersey Giants were doing wonderful, but then one day the smaller, Shirley, was dragging her head on the ground. It seemed to be a broken neck and I panicked at the idea that I would have to put her down...somehow. She only walked backwards and her head hung low. She came inside with me under watchful supervision. I made her a little neck brace with cotton balls and tape and held her on my lap to watch "American Idol." Two other cats joined Shirley on my lap and no one was the wiser of what I held in my hand. We placed her in a shoe box within the plastic box that night. Fully expecting her to be dead come dawn, I snuck out and noticed an empty shoe box. She had busted out of the neck brace and jumped out of the box to rejoin her sisters! I may have a new business on my hands. Neck braces for chickens! Weeks later everything seemed to be going well. The chickens were bigger and they were not staying in their plastic box much anymore. One day when Doug went in to feed them, another buff girl, limp and lifeless, lay near the box. It was sad.

Shirley succumbed to the wrath of the evil four year old neighbor a few months ago as well as one of the white girls (Lucy...Ethel is still here flying out of the coop!), and one of the buffs, Violet. I had prepared myself for coyotes, foxes, and raccoons, never a child and his dog. So, left with five we are anxious to bring in ten new little Velociraptors to join our team. I will still use the box technique but I need to figure out a way to keep the big girls away from the new babies. Without a mother hen there, they could be as detrimental to the babies as Zuzu the cat. I need to set up some kind of barrier, but what?

Well, a family of super sensitive, vegetarians survived our first year of loving and losing chickens and is ready for another group. We are hooked. Chicken farming seems to be our future. Crazy chicken antics, the delicious eggs and Laverne and Peep wanting attention all the time make it all worth it!

Chickens 101

I followed my friends around incessantly that first spring. Like a four year old I kept asking, "What is that?" "Why are they doing that?" "How do I do that?" "What do chickens eat?" "Where do chickens sleep?" Though I thought I knew the answer to that one, in their nests, silly. Geez. Wrong. My friends graciously answered my questions but after a while started just saying, "It's easy. There is nothing to it." And, really, it is very easy!

I am on a mission to inspire as many people as I can to get chickens. I am amazed at the ease of this endeavor and the pets that they have become. Like I have said before, in cities and counties all across the country (including Denver where you can have eight chickens!), people are being allowed the simple right to raise chickens. Even though we don't eat our chickens, the eggs have made an exceptional addition to our diet. The bright orange yolks and delicious whites of the egg brighten any recipe and since I don't buy factory farmed eggs, these eggs are like little gifts of gold each day! I am that much closer to my homesteading goals of self-sufficiency and I do save money by having my own eggs and selling the excess.

Choose Chickens - Early in the season you should head to the feed store and pick out your girls and place them on order. You could do mail order as well but since I have a feed store a few blocks away, I'll let them order the babies for me. This year I am getting Araucanas, Marans, and Buff Orpingtons. Like expecting parents, we are very excited! Araucanas lay Easter eggs, Marans lay dark chocolate eggs, and Buffs are lovey and cute and good layers. When we went to visit my friend she showed me her Marans. She let me hold and keep the most beautiful dark chocolate egg. I cradled it and stared at it in awe until Doug wryly said, "It's not real chocolate!"

Chicken Motel - Now you need a house for the chickies. You could build one, there are many great plans out there (thank goodness there was already one here!), or you can buy a ready-made one. The girls just need the house to lay eggs in and to sleep in. It's been so terribly cold here that I do feel sorry for the chickens down the block. They have a house that is three foot by one foot and it seems a little small when the ladies are inside more because of the cold. Ours is 10x10 and for only five chickens, it's a mansion. My friends use their shed as a coop. There really isn't a right or wrong way to house the girls. Just make sure they are safe, nothing can dig under or get through the door at night, and you are all set.

Chicken Beds and Nests- Apparently chickens do not sleep in their nests as cartoons falsely led me to believe. They sleep up higher in the coop. There is a shelf my girls sleep on, all huddled up together. I have seen some coops that have 2x4s to create little perches across the coop. I put down old, vintage vegetable crates for their nests. Carefully I designed their coop so they could lay eggs in style. They all lay in one corner, in between all of the cute boxes!

Chicken Food- We borrowed a feeder that you pour the feed in the top and it pours down into their tray. We still use that, it works well. I buy organic feed. No use feeding the girls genetically modified corn and who knows what else. It will transfer through the eggs to me and organic feed will keep the ladies and my family healthier. It is only a couple bucks more. A $25 a bag will last me about a month and a half. My piggy cats and dogs cost a lot more than that and they don't lay eggs!

Chicken Water- We borrowed a waterer that you fill upside down, then clumsily fasten on the bottom that serves as the water bowl, quickly turn it right side up as the water comes streaming into the ravine, curse as it wasn't really fastened and the water is all over your shoes, and carry the ton back to the chicken coop. I now use a mixing bowl. Yes, a mixing bowl. I keep it under their light so that the water doesn't freeze.

Chicken Bedding- I learned some very interesting things when I went to see Joel Salatin. One, I could not phantom why my coop smelled like cat boxes that hadn't been scooped in two weeks. Ammonia is not my favorite smell. It turns out that using straw creates this lovely aroma. That is all I had ever heard of or read about using! Pine shavings were recommended. They are cheap and a bag covers the whole coop floor. Now, instead of cleaning out the coop every few weeks as I was doing, one is supposed to leave it over the winter. Just keep adding on layers. The heat from the future compost helps keep the coop snug and the layers begin to break down so that by spring, when you dig out all the layers, you will have wonderful compost! Since the pine shavings don't break down as fast in the compost pile, I have now started layering; one month straw, the next month pine, and so forth. This will create a nice blend of nitrogen for my compost pile in the spring. On particularly cold days, the chickens will burrow into the bedding to keep warm.

Chicken Playground- The chickens have a fenced in area to keep them safe from predators. It is made from t-posts and chicken wire with bird netting on top when the snow isn't knocking it down. I think the best fencing if one can afford it is dog kennel fence. If a large dog can't get out of it, a large coyote can't get in! The girls need to wallow in the dirt. When I first saw this spectacle I thought Ethel was having a seizure. Apparently not, they just enjoy a good roll in the dirt. It gets the bugs off of them and gets them to lower areas of soil to find their favorite snack, bugs!

Now that you have a basic concept of how easy it would be to add chickens to your household and I have now helped you avoid annoying all your friends with rapid fire questioning, you are free to start finding chicken breeds! You're going to love them!

13 Chicken Myths the Ladies Would Like You to Know

Ethel, Laverne, Peep, Daffodil, and Mahalia would like to start the New Year by setting the record straight. There are a lot of funny misconceptions and misinformation out there about chickens. I know, because I believed every one of them, even Number 13, which was debunked for me just two days ago. Who started these ideas? Well, anyways, let's set the record straight!

1. Brown eggs are healthier than white eggs - Give a pat on the back to some executive out there; this was pure advertising genius making this up! Millions of brown eggs were sold in the hopes for better health! Turns out the color of the egg is determined by the color of the chicken's earlobe. Nothing else. So, Ethel, the California White, lays white eggs, the buffs lay brown eggs, and Laverne, who is all black with brown ear lobes, lays petite light brown eggs. This year we would like to get Araucanas for their green eggs.

2. Chickens need a rooster there in order to lay eggs - I get quite a few people who look confused when we say we don't have a rooster. "How do they lay eggs?" I think I may have asked this during the barrage of questions I followed my chicken friends around asking before I got my ladies. You need a rooster to fertilize the egg to make babies, but just like mammals, the egg cycle goes on, man or not.

3. Eggs go bad quickly - The eggs that you get at the grocery store were laid many weeks ago. They will stay good in the fridge for another few weeks. Farm fresh eggs have their natural coating on them (we don't wash ours until we are ready to use them and only if they really need it) so they will stay good on the counter for four weeks or so. Pretty impressive, huh? How to check for a bad egg- Place egg in a cup of water; if it floats throw it out, if it hovers in the middle, eat it right away, if it sinks, it is still nice and fresh.

4. The yolk is the baby - The yolk is the feed sack for the baby as its growing. He/she will use the yolk as nutrients and food until he busts out of his shell in search of other things. So, when you break into that delicious yolk, it was not going to become a baby!

5. Eggs from a factory farm are the same as the ones out of your coop - The chickens that lay eggs for the grocery stores are in tiny cages where they cannot get up or even turn around. They get their beaks lopped off so that when they go crazy (you would too in that situation) they don't hurt themselves or the chicken inches away from them. They eat genetically modified grain all day, no yummy plants. Whatever they eat, you eat when you eat the egg. Aggression and fear releases cortisol which transfers to the animal products we eat. Happy chickens running free in the back yard produce healthy, better tasting eggs!

6. It is difficult to have chickens - From Denver to New York and many cities in between are allowing coops to go up. Did you know that it was Martha Stewart who spearheaded the change in government policies so that she could have chickens? Chickens are no trouble at all. I let the girls out of the coop in the morning into their run or in the yard. I check their food and water and collect their eggs. At night, when the girls get tired and go into the coop to roost, I go close the door (and give kisses). I use organic chicken feed and it costs less than dog food.

7. Chickens are noisy - I know a lot of little dogs that create a lot more racket than chickens! They strut around and squawk when they lay an egg, or in the mornings when they want out of the coop, but otherwise, not a sound. They are deliberate creatures, looking for food in all places and don't have much time to talk. Roosters will crow several times a day but I am still at a loss as to why that is considered a nuisance in cities. I know many children and dogs considerably noisier. By the way another myth, "Roosters crow at dawn" is a deception too. They can crow at dawn, but they crow when they want to say something. I actually hear the guy's across the street at lunchtime more than dawn!

8. Chickens don't fly - Most do. Ethel flies wherever she sees fit while her devoted followers attempt but can't really get off the ground yet. Many chickens will roost in trees if you let them stay out in the summer. (Not recommended; invites chicken dinners!)

9. Chickens are dumb - The girls see me coming. If they hear the back door close they know I am about to open the coop and they start whooping and hollering. They run to their little chicken door to

go out. They jump up and down in front of the food. They are at least as smart as my Greyhound! Ethel finds every hole in the fence and the exact spot to fly out of the run. Peep has a bad habit of getting stuck in the snow. She runs to the bird feeders only to realize that the whole ground beneath is covered in icy snow. She jumps up on the bench and tries to figure out how to fly over the snow. Soon, she will turn towards the back door and starts squawking until I come out and get her to clearer ground.

10. A red dot in the egg means it is fertilized- Another beauty I was told at a health food store and believed until the occasional one popped up in my eggs, and there is no man in sight! It is simply a little bit of blood from a broken blood vessel when the egg was forming. It won't kill you and it's not a baby!

11. Roosters are mean - Just as some men can be mean, so can some roosters. But it would be unfair to say all men and roosters are bad! We love all the good ones! A rooster's job as the man of the coop is to protect the ladies. He keeps a sharp look out for predators and keeps the girls safe. If the rooster knows you, if you raised him from a peep, he could be as cuddly as a kitten. Some will take their job seriously and be more aloof. And there is a percentage that will be jerks. I would like a rooster though. I love their sweet crowing and I would love help keeping a lookout for chicken eaters!

12. Chickens love lush yards with lots of ornamental plants - My mother told me that the chicken run will be just dirt quickly. I wasn't sure until I saw it. The girls are so busy aerating the chicken run, that indeed, no plant will survive their tiny beaks and claws. However, the manure and its nitrogen will make a lovely garden if replanted. I keep an eye on the girls in the rest of the yard. They have done wonders for the ailing lilac bushes we inherited when we moved in. They have aerated and fertilized and the bushes are just bursting with new growth. The yard wasn't full of lush grass when we came in, so the ladies can't do too much damage but I make sure they don't concentrate on any one spot too long. If I keep them moving and they only graze the top layers and fertilize, the yard ought to look pretty good next year.

13 - And the one I just learned, a rooster can only make babies with the same breed- A rooster can make babies with any breed.

That is why there are cross breeds of chickens. So, make sure you get a breed of rooster with the qualities you want in a hen, good layers, cold hearty, etc. I think I may get an Araucana rooster. I am still researching and I still have much to learn!

The Quick Switch

Coyotes had wiped out eighteen of her chickens in a mere two eves. Only one remained. A docile Jersey Giant like our Laverne. We said we would take her. The coyotes, for some reason, gather chicken buffets from all around us, but have never ventured into our yard. (Let me go find some wood to knock on real quick....) Perhaps because we keep them locked up snug starting at dusk? A loving guard greyhound? Too much racket in the fairgrounds? Whatever the reason, we seem to have a little chicken shield around our place.

Laverne used to be a pair. Laverne and Shirley were a few of our first chickens but an accident involving a maniac four year old and his dog ended the life of Shirley. So, Doug deemed the new girl Shirley, as she is smaller than Laverne, and he just likes having Laverne and Shirley in the back yard. Now, how to get her in without anyone noticing?

We have failed at this before. The first time we introduced too soon in the daylight...not good. The second time we introduced ten chicks in a dog carrier over the course of three days. That worked fairly well, but the bully big girls were still pretty snotty. We had to think of a way to introduce a full grown chicken into the coop of fifteen residents without anyone being the wiser.

We had been told to introduce them overnight. Simply sneak the new girl in come the middle of the night and everyone wakes up with complete amnesia. Jill recommended that we rearrange their surroundings as well so they think they are in a new place all together. I still had a nervous feeling that we would wake to full blown chicken fighting come dawn. We had switched the dog kennel that was still in the coop with the one Shirley was in when we came home. We gave her food and water but left her door closed. After our movie ended late, we snuck out quietly into the coop, careful not to rouse the girls, as any time of day or night seems to be a good time to eat for them. We moved their food over there, their water over here, this moved there, and that over here, and opened Shirley's cage door, said a prayer, and went to bed!

This morning I shot out of bed at dawn when I heard Henry announcing his wake up call. I went to the coop. No one even noticed the petite brunette eating side by side or dust bathing. She and Laverne have already become buddies.

How Much Do You Feed Chickens?

I think I was starving my chickens. I am not proud of this. Further reason that I write about these things to educate folks on exactly how-to because I can never find the answers on these things until it hits me in the face!

When we first got chickens, we had eight. Three or so scoops two or three times a day to spoil them, lots of scraps, running around the yard, they were all set. We lost some, got some more, now at fifteen, upped the food ration some, everything seemed good. Lost some, gained some, now we are at twenty-four as of last August. Upped it a little (now at nine scoops a day, probably the equivalent to a cup and a half a scoop) and that is when I noticed as the girls (and rooster) got bigger over this autumn that they seemed more desperate. We blamed it on our move, then their molting. We noticed that the gate kept being opened to the chicken yard. We asked the neighbors, no one had touched it. We put a cinder block in front of the gate, they moved it. They, meaning twenty-four hysterical birds. They did indeed descend from dinosaurs.

I began to ask folks how much food we should be giving the chickens. They stopped laying eggs all together. They didn't look emaciated, but they certainly weren't happy. Sandy and Lisa both just fill up the feeders in their coops. Doug said the chickens will go through it in one day!

"Then they were hungry!" was Sandy's smart reply!

So, he filled up the two foot high feeder. And it was half gone the first day. But since then it has leveled off and we were indeed starving our chickies and we feel terrible about that. Sandy also mentioned that throwing out a bowl full of scratch daily is added protein and food.

We read several articles and books. None of them ever mentioned just filling the feeders up. In fact, I have read that you don't free feed because they will just eat and eat and eat. I also read that you don't keep a heat lamp on or they get "weak" and that if the power went out on a cold night they wouldn't be used to it and would die. I have read all sorts of things, but here is the conclusion that this farmer has come up with.

Free feed, particularly in the winter. They aren't able to run around and find bugs and such. They need more food in the winter to keep warm. They produce eggs for me which is food for me. They deserve fresh water, treats, and plenty of food. They deserve a red light in the coop. It was negative twenty-two degrees last night. We turned on the lamp! They may not be pets in the sense that the cats are, but they are still in my care and on my farm and should receive the exact same care and treatment as the indoor animals. I free feed the cats and dogs, why not the chickens?

I hate learning farming lessons the hard way but then at least I can help out a new chicken person when they ask, "How much do I feed my chickens?"

Ducks

Waddling, quacking, swimming, bug eaters and comedians.

For the Love of Ducks!

Wouldn't that be a fabulous exclamatory sentence? "For the love of ducks, get in here!!" I might start using that.

I have been talking about getting ducks for years. I have researched them and coveted them. Nancy had some ducks this year that she inherited. They were called Chocolate Runners. They looked like Walt Disney himself designed them. They looked like bowling pins, slightly slanted, running about in a pack. They were so comical and so mesmerizing, Doug and I could not keep from giggling as we watched them.

So, my questions and concerns about ducks:

1. They are supposedly noisy. I have tested out my neighbors though and they seem to be immune to a barking dog, bleating goats, humming alpacas, clucking chickens, and an uproariously loud opera singer named Henry the Rooster. I think they can take a few quacking ducks.

2. Do they need their own coop? I only have one. They get into water and may make a mess of the water bowl. However, the chicken water bowl is my mixing bowl stolen from the kitchen. (The dog has one, the cats have one, I really do need new mixing bowls!) So, they can't make that much of a mess! I was told today at the feed store that they do eat pine shavings which is less than good for them and that I will need to use straw, which is more odorous, but I suppose I can change it more.

3. Where am I going to get a pond? I live in town for duck's sake. We talked about getting the water feature in the yard fixed that has long been out of use. It was rotted, holey, and non-working when we moved in. A child's swimming pool in that area though could work. The gal at the feed store said my chickens will drown. She underestimates the intelligence of my chickens.

4. What the heck do they eat? There is mixed flock poultry feed but layer feed is sufficient. They eat a lot though.

5. Are they going to catch sight of the fairgrounds and fly south? Apparently Runner ducks like Nancy's can only fly three feet up so they aren't going very far. Other breeds can have a few feathers clipped with sharp scissors on one side and that takes care of that.

6. How many eggs do they lay? Cause I have enough free loaders around here. Duck eggs fetch $8 a dozen at the nearby farmers markets. Depending on the duck breed, they can lay anywhere from 50-330 eggs per year. The meat breeds don't lay as many. Runner ducks range between 150-300 eggs per year. More than some of the chickens I have.

Feeling confident, I went to the feed store and pre-ordered my ducks. Two blue Runners and two chocolate Runners. Straight run. Eek. I asked what if they are all boys? I can bring them to the animal swap if I don't want to kill them myself, the clerk says.

Folks, I cannot even put my old, decrepit, eighteen year old dog to sleep for crying out ducks. How am I going to butcher my ducks? I will pray for all girls.

I can leave them in the same coop as the chickens. I can put the swimming pool out by the old water feature and hope the chickens don't drown.

Or, I can put them in the goat yard with their own coop. Maybe there is one on Craig's List. They can run around with the goats, have their swimming pool, and I can hope the goats don't break into their food. I can totally see the goats chowing down on duck feed.

I have until April 11th to figure it out. The ducks arrive then. This is becoming more of a farm every year!

Chicks and Ducks (the first six weeks)

The mini-quacking from the chicken coop cannot help but bring a smile to my face. The ducklings are so amazingly adorable. The chicks are cute running around in hysteria. Yes, the babies have been moved to the coop with just a little worry on my part. Last year we were absolutely paranoid when we transferred the new chicks to the coop. The hens look larger than life when you compare them to six week old chicks! They also seem angry. But we have found a way to do this successfully each time.

From 1 day old through four weeks old they destroy the bathroom. The bathtub is safe, weather free, continuously warm, and dry (except for the ducks). We set up a plastic tub in the bathtub with a little straw, their feeder and a cup of water. We attach the heat lamp rather low, just above the box. We dip each chick's beak into the water to get them drinking. We check for poopy bottoms that need to be cleaned (just yank it off) the first couple of weeks. We see if the chicks are huddled under the light (too cold) or in the far corner (too hot) and adjust the lamp from there. The chicks should be running around. Raise the lamp a little each week.

There are only two adversaries of a bathtub chick; cats that can get through the door (thankfully no issues here), and an open toilet seat. I am afraid one chick could not swim. She hadn't even flown out of the box yet when Emily found her. How did she get over there?! Conspiracy theories fill our heads.

On their fourth week birthday the bathtub is again available for use. The chicks move to the garage. We bought a large metal portable fence rather inexpensively at the farm store. It folds up or out and becomes whatever size you need. A folding table covered the top with about a foot open on one end to allow the heat lamp to shine through. We made sure the birds were comfortable and loud. Sure sign of happy chicks.

On their fifth week birthday the whole contraption moves inside the chicken coop. The chicks (and ducks) stay in the cage for another week while the ladies get used to them being there and their ruckus.

On their sixth week birthday night we propped the door open a few inches. That way they can come out and run in but the big girls cannot get into the cage. The next morning at the crack of dawn I was out there checking to make sure there were no massacres. No one seems the wiser and the interest is in food and freedom. While the hens are out running around enjoying the lawn and the day, the chicks and ducklings wander the coop. They will at some point discover their way out only to have to be corralled back in when they cannot figure out reentry. It is one of our jobs here, rounding up chicks. Not a bad gig. They will eventually grow even bigger and be a part of the flock before we know it.

Discovering a Drake

We've been watching Irene for a while. She has a zigzag on her chest that makes her look like a superhero and she stands much taller and bigger than the other ducks. Some women are built that way. I wasn't judging. They follow her everywhere. She enjoys a good swim in their child sized swimming pool as well as leisurely walks about the farm with her friends in tow.

Yesterday, Sylvia, who has a profound permanent limp (if she turns out to be a boy I shall call her Tiny Tim) decided to envelop herself in the thicket of lilacs and have a bit of a nap. Head tucked backwards into her feathers she slept peacefully beneath the leafy arc. Irene was beside herself. All three ducks quacking and looking for their friend. They went under the porch, then came back out. They called far and away and close by. Beneath the table, in the pool, in the coop, around the tree they paraded and called. Finally, sleepy Sylvia awoke and ran out of the lilacs to meet her friends who quickly ran towards her, all of them quacking at once.

That was when I noticed it. Irene has a real raspy voice, like an old time jazz singer that has been smoking too long. And the tell tail sign (literally) was the curly tail. At just about four months, we did not see it before this week. Suddenly her sweet feminine tail feathers curled into a tight ringlet. Irene is a boy.

I do hope that Irene, I mean Ira, will behave himself with the females.

Just Duckie

Last year I took some pretty darn cute photos of our ducklings. They were so soft and added quite a lot of smiles at the Easter dinner table when I let one run across. Three inch high ducklings are a force to be reckoned with in the ridiculously adorable animal category.

They were a mess. They loved to splash. They loved to get their water everywhere, in the food, in the straw, all over themselves and the patient chicks they were housed with. (I think those chicks thought themselves to be ducks.) Finally at five weeks old, the whole crew was placed in the chicken coop in a portable fence so that they could get to know their roommates before running for their life from the older hens.

Doug placed a kiddie swimming pool outside and they spent hours and hours delighting in the water and splashing enthusiastically. Not always swimming, sometimes they would stand outside the pool with their head in the water. As they got older we noted that three were female and we had one male. One drake out of four straight run fowl isn't bad. I could have as easily had three drakes and one sole girl! He was their protector and would only allow the three chickens that they had been raised with to be near them.

We would come home from a farmer's market and our intern, Ethan, would casually say, "Ira had Yetta's head in his mouth again."

"Ira had Sophia's head in his mouth again." He didn't hurt them but we weren't sure what the future would bring.

Well, what it brought was a move. A move we had been praying for and that I had been writing about for two solid years. The move to our homestead. More land, more opportunity. Lots of room for animals, right? We moved in the fall during our peak of garden production, farmer's markets, then transplanting herbs to the new farm, and a strenuous move. There wasn't time to build a separate coop for the ducks and we still didn't know if we were going to let the chickens free range outside their enclosure due to the significant large bird population that lived nearby (owls and hawks don't mind free chicken). We could hear coyotes singing in the fields (they like a bit of chicken as well). And Ira with a chicken in his mouth. No, no, that would never do. We couldn't keep them all cooped up together any longer. So, I sold them for a very low price (as I am so prone to do). They went to live next door to my friend, Lisa. I mourned their absence immediately. I did love the ducks.

So now spring is approaching and I have BIG plans. Do I plan any other way? So we (when I say we, I mean Doug) is going to build a jaunty fenced in run along the west side of the garden where the majority of grasshoppers seemed to be last fall. The ducks will have a job! West border bug patrol, duck manure for the compost, and fresh eggs for the cast iron skillet. They will have their own digs, their own kiddie pool, and their own small coop. Now, I sure hope I don't get three drakes and one duck egg layer. Let's go for all four girls!

I miss their quacking on an early summer morning. Their humorous waddles across the grass. The sound of water splashing and raucous playing. A farm without farm animals is simply a garden. I love my gardens and the farm we are creating here and I need my Noah's Arc menagerie to make it complete.

Goats

Like puppies, only they stay outdoors and produce yummy milk. They do like to watch television and go on car rides

Goats 101

Our alpaca venture failed miserably, with a great financial loss, and two stubborn alpacas now working as lawn mowers somewhere in Limon. I had to give them away. I do love our chickens. I adore the ducks. I love goats. I am smitten.

Our adventure started badly enough, a doe that wouldn't come near us, would sit in the milk bucket, and give us dirty looks. Katrina is so happy in her new home though, surrounded by baby goats, chickens, little kids, and even lets her new mom milk her without a stanchion!

Our other doe loved us tremendously, following us like a lost puppy, always wanting to help and snuggle. She died in March giving birth. Yet, our hearts were still in the game. We were ready to be goat herders.

Elsa was a gift from my goat guru, Jill, after Loretta's death. Jill had to move shortly after and also offered me Elsa's mom, who is our milker around here. Gentle and sweet, she is the perfect goat. Amy and Rob adopted Katrina's doeling that was born on the farm and adopted three others from Jill and have been boarding them here. Six caprine comedians taking up residence. They are a delight. I highly recommend getting goats.

Here are some things you may want to know when contemplating becoming a goat herder.

1. What kind of goat?

Fainting goats and pigmy goats are very good companions for horses and other pack animals that may get lonely in a large pasture. They are fun to watch and are incredibly, ridiculously cute. However, they are not really great as milkers and pigmies have issues giving birth. They are more pet status than anything else.

Nigerian Dwarves make really great goats in the city. Denver and Colorado Springs now allow small goats, which Dwarves qualify as. They are a sturdy, fun-loving breed. They can give a quart or two a day of fresh, raw goat's milk, perfect for a family homestead.

Alpines, Saanens, Oberhasli, and Nubians are great milkers. Large in stature (Isabelle is bigger than our greyhound), they have large udders and drop twins and triplets often. Nubians have higher milk fat in their milk which makes very creamy cheese. Turns out Dwarves have the highest milk fat but you would need four days of milk to get enough to make a good block of cheddar!

We started with Dwarves because they were easier to handle in my mind. We ended up with a purebred Saanen and her daughter who is half Saanen and half Alpine. They are very easy to handle. I am coveting Amy and Rob's Alpine that lives here. She looks like a Siberian husky and is gorgeous and adorably sweet. I would also like a Nubian.

Expect to pay anywhere from free (if someone is desperate because they are moving) to $200 for a non-registered goat and between $200 to upwards of $800 for papered, purebred kids.

Always get two. They are pack animals and cannot live in singles.

2. What About Disbudding?

The memory of the bad goats at our friends' house that we were babysitting stayed with me. Pinned against a metal stock fence calling for Doug and having my hip bone repeatedly rammed and watching Doug get butted in the stomach made me not want large goats at all. Especially goats with horns! All my other friends disbud their goats. Seems mean, hold down a two week old goat kid while they scream bloody murder and set a hot curling iron looking thing to their horn nubs and burn it off! But, on closer inspection, it is actually not what it seems. Jill's goat guru (do you think I will ever be called that?), Brittney, disbuds all of ours. She told us why they are screaming; because they are prey animals and being held down means they are about to be eaten. You'd be screaming bloody murder too. The burning is only on the hard, nerveless horn endings and takes about ten seconds. Done. It doesn't touch the skin and two seconds later the goat kids are running around playing again. I appreciate not having horns stabbed into my hip if someone wants to play, or having them stuck in the fence.

3. What Do They Eat?

Goats like a diet of pure alfalfa flakes supplemented with pastures of weeds. Actually their favorite is trees. They love giant, green, taunting limbs of leaves. And tree bark. After the trees are gone, they will reluctantly munch on weeds. It is a fallacy that goats eat everything. One would be surprised to know that they are rather finicky eaters. They will eat about three quarters of the hay you set before them, sigh, and wander off to find a nice bush sticking through the fence from the neighbor's yard. They do not eat tin cans, or odds and ends.

They should also be supplemented (this can be set out in small bowls to free feed) minerals and baking soda. Minerals they are missing and baking soda to get rid of bloat. They will help themselves as needed.

Lots of fresh water is imperative, of course.

4. Playtime

Goats love a good time. We have several discarded tires that are stacked up along with an old, rusty keg. Doug calls it Mount Kegle. It is a playground of fun (and used to reach the higher branches of trees). Goats are really fun to watch play. They head-butt (good thing they are disbudded) and jump 360's off of wood piles and feeding troughs. One night Doug was in the pasture with them at dusk. Goats are particularly silly at dusk. He would run across the yard then stop and turn to look at them. All at once they would all rear up and start hopping on all fours like giant bunny rabbits....sideways towards him! It was the funniest thing I have seen in a long time.

5. Pasture Rotation

We are in a fine, old fashioned back yard so how we do pasture rotation is by fencing off half the yard. They stay on one side for three weeks, and then move to the other. This allows the grass to start growing back.

6. Housing

I bought a simple igloo for the goats as their house on one side of the yard. The old alpaca shelter consists of a covering between the chicken coop and the garage. It keeps the rain out and there is a gate on one side. Goats do not need an entire barn. The igloo is weather proof and kept rather warm even on our below zero days and nights last winter. They enjoy sleeping outdoors when the weather is nice.

7. Breeding

Boys are smelly when they get older. When they want to get it on they pee on their faces and let loose an oily substance on their skin that makes them irresistible to the opposite sex (of goat). Lord, they are maniacs. So, we will rent a man. Jill knows of the perfect date for Elsa and Isabelle come late fall and either they will visit him or he shall come here and we will have a rendezvous and come spring will hopefully have adorable new babies around. Dwarves should not be bred their first year. That is what happened with Loretta (on accident). Only the large breeds can have sex as teenagers. The Dwarves need to wait a year.

8. Fencing and Keeping Them In.

Last year's babies were out running down the street, eating the neighbor's grass, and running through the fairgrounds during a rodeo. We had the fence reinforced with smaller field fencing before this new bunch arrived. Twila was being terrible to the little ones, as she usually is, so we put her in the other yard. A split second later she cleared a four foot fence and was back with the little ones.

"How do you keep a goat in?" I asked Jill before this whole goat herding thing started. She replied that if a goat wants out, there is no stopping it. If they are happy, they will stay put. I have friends that use six foot fences, some electrified, watch for holes, and things that they can use as spring boards. We have a three-and-a-half, some places four foot, fence of field fencing. The kids stay put. There was a new hole in one though the other day and Doug asked real casual like, "Why is Tank in your potatoes?" The chubby baby goat didn't wait around to see if anyone was coming to fix the fence, he just wanted those potatoes! Be vigilant but also know that they will and can outsmart you if they wish. Just give them more tires and a lot of hugs.

I am by no means an expert yet. I am learning by trial and error, from my goat gurus, and from lots of books. The goats teach me most of all. Goats, as with every other creature on earth, are all very different. Each one has a unique personality. We have found a whole new layer of joy by becoming goat folks.

Get Your Goat! (A Love Story)

We loved goats after meeting one at a petting zoo while we still lived in the city. After being butted and bruised and bullied by our friend's goats while pet sitting we questioned whether we still wanted goats. Her goats were rescues, males, had horns, and were not wethered (neutered). We looked like good candidates for wrestling, apparently. So, we thought maybe all big goats were like that and wanted as small of ones as we could find.

We met babies at Nancy's for the first time and fell in love. Then we were directed to Jill who had the smallest, most adorable baby goats. They were Nigerian Dwarves. We gave in to our long time hopes for goats.

She gave us two goats that were half Dwarf. They were a huge hit at the farmer's market and an adorable addition to our farm, but they were little escape artists and loved to prance under the storming feet of the horses in the fairgrounds, or nose around our neighbor's garage for spilt chemicals. We sadly gave them back to Jill before they could get hurt.

Then she gave us two more dwarves, each pregnant, the younger one was the sweetest animal you can imagine. The older one had her baby, who we sold to our friends, and then the mom went to live with a family in Colorado Springs because she liked them better than us. The younger one died in child birth and broke our hearts.

Jill, in her unending generosity gave me yet another goat. Elsa Maria, who went to schools with me when I spoke, went to the library, the coffee shop, and Walmart. She loved to snuggle and sit on my lap. (I think she would still like that, but now it would be like a Rottweiler sitting on me, but more wiggly.) She brightened our home. Jill had to move and gave me Elsa's mother, Isabelle, who patiently let us learn to milk her and was a great companion to Elsa.

We boarded four goats. We have visited countless caprines and I must say we are definitely goat people.

Now we just have Isabelle and Elsa (who are Saanens, one of the largest breeds), who are each expecting and will increase our little herd by trading one of their doelings for a newborn Nubian that our friend is expecting. We loved having goat milk shares available, making our own cheese, and having these sweet, gentle creatures as companions. Goats do make a farm.

Five Reasons to Get Your Goat:

1. Farm Pets - These animals are like having an outdoor puppy all the time. Any time you can give is most welcome for snuggling, petting, getting them wound up and watching them hop around. You could pull up a lawn chair and watch the comedy show if you liked. Goats are ever the comedians. You can add a little happiness to the farm. Goats are becoming more and more welcome across the country. Big cities, including Denver and Colorado Springs, welcome small breeds of goats. Many places with HOA's don't. Don't move there, folks. It's not worth it.

2. Farm Products - In the spirit of everyone must pull their weight; goats are excellent at doing so. There are fiber goats that can give the farmer lovely threads, dairy goats that produce delicious milk (and cheese, yogurt, ice cream...), and, well, here on this little farm we have no meat animals, but let it be said that there are goats bred for meat too. Male goats can be used for breeding, or wethers can be used for companionship or protection of the herd. Babies can be used in place of Prozac.

Farm money can be made from selling said fibers, milk, dairy products, or babies.

3. Easy to Care For - Goats don't require too much in the way of care. They like a couple flakes of hay a day, some minerals and baking soda in a dish, and sweet feed during milking. Fresh water and bedding. A good fence. The adage goes though, "If a goat isn't happy, nothing will keep it in." So, keep your girls happy and they should stay put but a good field fence is wise. They need their toenails trimmed and some good herbal medicines at the ready if needed but outside of that, they require little more than a few hugs.

4. Lawn Mowers - Goats do love a good bite to eat (don't we all?) and they would like to eat whatever you place them on. They will not eat everything as the rumors would say but they like grasses and

weeds. Oh, and trees. Don't let them near the trees you want to keep unless it is large and quite established! They will mow down a grassy area so that you don't have to.

5. Shock and Smile Factor - Have you ever walked down the street with a goat on a leash? No?! Oh my, you don't know what you are missing. Traffic slows or stops, people point, take second looks, question slowly if it is a dog, and it brings countless smiles to stranger's faces.

Goats equal Happiness!

Bottle Feed or Leave on Mom?

Starting out I watch my friends, read books, ask questions, and then tried to make my own way. Whether to leave the baby on the mother or bottle feed was no exception.

Jill takes the baby from the mother immediately. She gives the baby bottles of colostrum for a few days then off they go with their perspective owner or stay with her bottle feeding for ten or so weeks. The mothers truly forget what they were doing. They can be in the same pen with the infant and have no maternal urge to nurse or protect the youngster. On the same note, the baby thinks that the bottle feeder is her mom and is happy as can be playing with the other goats and drinking bottles. Her goats are super friendly (Loretta was a bottle baby, and so is Elsa) and excited to see people. More like small dogs, they are playful and love attention.

Nancy leaves the baby on the mom. After three weeks she separates them at night, milks in the morning, and then lets the baby stay with the mom all day. She gets plenty of milk, and then doesn't have to worry about bottle feeding, weaning, or anything but once a day milking. The babies are nice enough, though they do prefer to stay with their mom, which seems quite natural. Nancy slaughters some of them for meat. She has a full circle farm. Bottle babies become a part of the family, it would be difficult to eat a baby that you kept in the house and watched American Idol with.

When Katrina had her baby, Buttercup, I opted for Nancy's approach. Wasn't it mean to take away the baby from the mother? Wouldn't it be easier to milk in the mornings since we are just getting started? Wouldn't the baby be healthier if I left her on the mom? Buttercup is adorable, and as she gets bigger, she gets faster. The family that bought her comes to visit often. At the beginning, we could swoop the small infant up and snuggle her, but now we have to plan and coordinate her capture. She is like a feral cat. Her mother, who was already ornery, is now a beast with her infant by her side. She charged Bumble, the greyhound, and pushed him into a fence. He is a rather docile creature and easily injured. He did not understand why he was being attacked. He looked at me with big humane society eyes. The second time she was charging full speed towards him, thankfully, Doug was there to grab her collar and curtail her attempts at maiming the dog.

I discussed my issues about milking with Jill. Because Katrina is nursing all day, she doesn't let all her milk down for us. She is also a Nigerian Dwarf so has less milk anyway. Nancy has Nubians, so she gets plenty of milk. With a baby by her side, Katrina is not friendly. Milking time is no exception as she kicks, spills the milk bucket, and tries to get away. She sits down and thrashes about. She is a nightmare. If she didn't have a baby that would relieve her of her engorgement soon, she might be more apt to let us milk. Maybe.

Elsa is a bottle baby. She doesn't miss nor does she remember her mother who is happily getting milked twice a day. Elsa is excited for bottles and is content playing in the yard or sitting on my lap. She is growing steadily by the day and is more certain on her long legs. She enjoys sleeping on my lap alongside my cat while we watch singing shows in the evening. She doesn't seem overly traumatized from the experience of bottle feeding and lack of caprine matriarchal care. I seem to be a fine substitute. Elsa went and visited 119 middle school children yesterday at the schools I was speaking at. She was lovey and adorable, a great ambassador to the future farming world for some of these children, with any luck. There is no way we could have taken Buttercup.

The notion of bottle feeding goat kids being a nuisance is no longer contemplative. It is one of my greatest joys in farming.

With this small of a farm, I have to be choosy about what animals I have here. I have to consider that I do not have a lot of animals. I do not have a pack of goats or alpacas or sheep that sit out in a pasture all day. We have a sixth of an acre in each pasture. Our farm here was set up to be an example that one can farm anywhere, as a place where kids can come out and see vegetables growing, find eggs, and pet the goats. A place that may inspire them to have farms of their own when they get older. An aloof goat does nothing for atmosphere! This is also a homestead, and a place where I spend much of my time. I prefer very friendly animals. Even my chickens enjoy being picked up!

I am sure there are many situations where leaving the baby on the mother is beneficial and necessary on many farms, but for our small piece of friendly farm, as I sit writing this with a baby goat on my lap, bottle babies will be in our future.

Bottle Feeding Goats (a handy schedule)

When we got our first baby goats last summer, I had no idea how often to bottle feed a kid. There was nothing in books. Nothing on internet searches. I ended up texting my friend, Jill, every week to see what the new ration should be.

This year was no different. I couldn't remember how much to give each age and with Amy and Rob's goats here we had three babies on three schedules. We had their bottle feeding schedule written on the blackboard door. Instead of a burden, it was truly an act of love and instant happiness bottle feeding the babies.

The babies are finally weaned and the bottles go up for another year. I thought it might be helpful for other new parents of goats to have a feeding schedule. Also, when I forget, I can revert back to this schedule and see for myself how much each monster gets!

I had to call Jill one more time to find out about colostrum. She has always given me the babies post-colostrum feedings. She filled me in and we will be ready next year when Isabelle and the new babies start giving birth.

Day 1-2 Colostrum. Colostrum is the milk that all mommies produce the first few days. It is not like the milk we think of, but rather filled with immunities and nutrients to get the little babies off to a good start. Milk the mom immediately after she gives birth if it wasn't too difficult of a birth. Have some colostrum in the freezer (you can purchase it from another goat farmer if needed) to have on hand just in case.

4 ounces of colostrum should be heated up and given to the new baby every 2 hours around the clock. If they want more, they can have more at the feeding. This is the most important of all their feedings and they need as much as they will take.

Now starts our weeks:

Week 1 - Post-colostrum. 6 oz. of milk every 4 hours. Feed late in the evening and then early in the morning. No more midnight feedings! (Five times a day)

Week 2 - 8 oz. of milk every 6 hours. (Four times a day)

Week 3- 10 oz. of milk every 8 hours. (Three times a day)

Week 4 - 10 oz. of milk twice a day.

Week 5 - 10 oz. of milk once a day (this is when they start to get really nervous.)

Week 6 - Weaned. Treat if you feel really bad but they don't need any more bottles now. They should have noticed the other goats eating and be eating hay by now. A touch of sweet feed as a treat starting at 3 weeks helps entice them to eat solid foods.

Sadly put bottle up and wait until next year!

Milking 101 (and a word on raw milk)

I had milked a goat when I was nineteen working at an animal shelter that happened to have taken in a goat. Looking back it seemed very easy and I don't remember any issues. So when we got Katrina I thought it would come back to me. Of course Katrina wouldn't let her milk down and I had no idea where to squeeze on her giant Dwarf udder. A friend came to our rescue and showed us how to milk her. We were so thrilled with our half a cup of milk each day, that is if we could keep her from kicking the pail and making us lose all that precious coffee creamer. She supposedly had perfect udders but it didn't help me because I left the baby on and she really had no desire to share with me. I sold her and her new mama milks her without a milk stanchion and gets a quart a day! She just wasn't meant to be mine.

Jill gave us Isabella Noni, our giant Saanen who gives a gallon a day of delicious, creamy milk. Jill warned us that her udders were not great. They seemed like heaven to us after trying to milk Katrina. I did soon figure out why I couldn't milk very well after watching another gal milk her Nubians. She continued a conversation with us, not even looking at the bucket as she milked these goats so fast that I thought we were in a contest at the fair. She has smaller hands than I do....and then it hit me. Once Doug gets part of the milk out of the udder on Isabella it is then small enough for me to wrap my hand around. So, Elsa may be even easier to milk next year! I am glad we started out with the hardest animals and are working our way to the easiest. If we don't give up, we are in for rewards!

I would have loved a tutorial before I started milking, so I am demonstrating one here just in case a homesteader out there gets a goat that needs to be milked and thinks they can just wing it like we did!

First wash the udders lightly with a mixture of mild soap (like Dr. Bronner's) and water. I use a slip of paper towel because that is what I saw another girl do.

Oh, before that make sure she is locked into the stanchion happily munching away on sweet feed. Sweet feed looks like it was dipped in molasses and smells great. It provides mama with minerals and nutrients she needs while she is making all that milk. We had asked the people we used to get feed from for sweet feed and brought home regular goat feed. No wonder Katrina hated us. Make sure you have sweet feed!

The washing of her udders also gives her the hint that she needs to let the milk down. Wrap your thumb and forefinger around the upper part of the udder. Then close the other fingers letting your fingers come into a fist. Your hand doesn't move up or down. Do not pull! Then keep squeezing all that good milk out until not much is coming out and she is looking pretty shriveled. If she seems to be getting chapped, add a little skin salve or a touch of olive oil. Give her a kiss and a good pat on the head and repeat the whole thing twelve hours later.

Bring the milk into the kitchen. I like the two quart canning jars to put milk in because they are pretty but you could certainly refill old milk jugs, juice containers, or whatever. Put a funnel on top of the jar, then a strainer, then a square of tightly woven cheese cloth and strain the milk through. We were using coffee filters and they took the whole morning to strain through (I might be exaggerating but honestly, I haven't the patience for it that early). Then we tried just the sieve. It let a bit of hay through. Then the cheese cloth and it works just right.

Label the lid with the date because in the fridge they all look the same. Goat's milk stays good for about ten days. If it starts smelling sour use it to make soap, cheese, or take a bath in it. Chickens love it too. Goat's milk is homogenized, meaning it doesn't separate like cow's milk. This means it is a pain to make butter out of but a beauty to drink because it is super creamy and delicious. We recommend chocolate syrup. Cold chocolate milk is amazingly delicious.

A word on raw verses pasteurized. Louis Pasteur at the end of his life even questioned his theory. Once you pasteurize it, you kill it. There are no enzymes left to digest it leaving many folks with lactose intolerance issues and many others with gas and mucous problems. Raw milk has all the enzymes and nutrients intact. It helps the body to better absorb calcium, whereas pasteurized milk leaches calcium from the bones. E coli worry? Wash the udders. Do you know what the goat is eating? We use fresh alfalfa and organic sweet feed.

Clean water, lots of fresh air, and places to play. These are happy goats. My goats don't have parasites. I am not sure why the news is jumping on all things natural lately, I guess the organic, natural, farm movement is taking money from the big corporations, but I will keep on drinking raw milk because I know how I feel when I drink it. I know that it is good for my granddaughter to supplement her breast milk. Goat's milk is what our grandmas fed to infants if they couldn't breast feed. Have you read the ingredients for baby formula?

For the love of goats! I will get off my podium and encourage you to go get your milking goat. There is chocolate milk and hilarious goat antics waiting for your enjoyment.

Homemade Goat Cheese

I love the tangy, delicious flavor of soft goat cheese, often called Chevre, which is French for "goat". It is so easy to make and yields a lot more than one would get from the store. It is versatile enough that it can virtually match any dish. Herbs can be added, thick ribbons of basil, clips of chives, oregano, and green onion, a dash of red wine vinegar or lemon juice, and a good pinch of salt makes an amazing cheese to spread on crackers or fresh baked bread.

Adding a little more of the whey to create a creamier cheese allows it to be dressed up in Italian seasonings, a splash of lemon juice, and salt, and used in place of ricotta which creates an amazing flavor profile when added to pasta and rich tomato sauce. I added red wine, Italian seasonings, and garlic to my creamy cheese and baked it with ziti and spaghetti sauce. Amazing.

In this one I made it a bit sweeter than I typically do. It is fantastic with its sweet and slightly sour flavor. It is wonderful spread on breakfast toast or sprinkled on fresh salad greens. I added a teaspoon of vanilla salt and poured ginger peach syrup (a failed jam attempt) over the top. Very good.

You can make this with store bought goat's milk, or indeed substitute cow's milk, but we prefer fresh from the goat, raw milk. Nothing tastes as good as really fresh cheese.

Pour one gallon of milk into a stainless steel pot. Heat, stirring often, to 86 degrees. I use a laser thermometer.

Sprinkle on a packet of cultures. These are the ready-made cultures that we need to make a variety of cheeses. They are available at cheese supply websites but I get ours from the local homesteading store (Buckley's in Colorado Springs) or the local brew hut (Dry Dock in Aurora) that sells beer and wine making supplies. They sell cheese making supplies as well.

Let sit for 2 minutes to rehydrate then stir into milk.

Place a cover on the pot and let it set for 12 hours. I do this so that it can sit overnight.

In the morning line a colander with cheesecloth. To help keep me from cussing, I use clothes pins to secure it to the sides of the colander as I pour. I have a pot beneath the colander to catch the whey. This will be used in bread baking or to add a bit more liquid to my finished cheese if desired.

Pour the contents of the pot through the cheesecloth and catch all that fabulous cheese. Tie the cheesecloth (I use clothespins to secure) and either attach it to the side of the pot to drain or tie it and hang it from somewhere to drain for 4-8 hours depending on how dry you want your cheese. I like 4 hours.

At that point, I refrigerate the whey, place the cheese in a container, and start seasoning. Enjoy! There are beneficial enzymes in goat cheese that are important to our digestive health. Goat cheese spread on crackers or fresh bread, a glass of wine, and a book beneath a tree. One of the great pleasures of summer!

Drying Off Isabelle (and new boyfriends)

I am a tad envious of those raised on a farm. They don't have to text random people that have goats to ask stupid questions. Like, how the heck do we stop her milk? I know this should seem like an obvious one but there is an art to all this dairy farming. Goodness, we don't want to send our goat into pain, discomfort, mastitis, and who knows what else! Our dear Isabelle trusts us.

I first started by looking up on the internet how to dry off a goat. Easy. Just start milking once a day, then every other day, then every third day, etc. We easily got her down to once a day. That was great for weeks but we don't have any CSA's anymore and I stopped making cheese for the season so five cups of milk a day is a little overkill. It certainly fills the fridge up quickly. I have been avidly making eggnog, but even then, I still have a lot of milk in there. The freezer is full of milk and neither of us wants to go out in the freezing cold to milk so even though we could wait until her third month of pregnancy to dry her off, we have opted to give us all a much needed respite.

We then waited a day before milking her. Her udder was hard as a rock and Doug's hands were getting tired getting all the milk out. You think I am sappy and sensitive? My husband is worse. He loves these creatures and wants them to experience zero discomfort. So we were back to once a day again.

I finally asked a random goat person how to dry off a goat. She told me the same thing we had already learned so we just went for it. Every other day. Check, less milk. Every third day. The next time we milk will be Friday which is the fourth day. She has not been engorged since that first time. All it took was that first bit of pressure to send the message to her body to ease up on the milk production.

On Sunday, Isabelle has a hot date. We ought to put a nice red flower in her hair or something. You know, distract from the beard. She is going to his house because we are having trouble figuring out when she is in heat and the hour and a half drive the second we find out she is in heat would be difficult. So instead she is having a slumber party until she gets pregnant. Don't judge. She makes really cute babies. Her own baby, Elsa, will be bred this year too. Since goats are pack animals, they will go together. A few weeks without goats, that will be strange! We'll miss them.

Part 4 (Preserving; Creating a very convenient grocery store.)

Canning (Not as scary as it sounds!)

Canning Sweet Corn

I cannot emphasize enough how important it is to learn to can. It seems that it skipped a generation and very few people my age even know how to can. Folks think it is easier to buy food from the store. I disagree. How many hours does one have to work in order to buy food? I would rather spend those hours in the garden or at the farmer's market. In just a few hours one can turn an entire bag of corn into several jars of delicious sweet corn, summer flavor locked in, to enjoy all winter. It is a rather nice task with huge rewards.

Not only do you know where your food is coming from, how it was raised, how long ago it was harvested, how big the footprint is, and if it is organic, but you also provide yourself food security. Big snow storm? No job? Car broke down? Can't get to the store? No problem. The grocery store is in the basement.

I am not growing enough to can yet. Each stalk will produce 1-2 good ears of corn. I got a big bag of corn from Miller Farms (they are not certified organic, but I know for a fact that they do not use pesticides, fertilizers, or any kind of herbicide. They also use non-GMO corn) and went to work.

1. Shuck a big bag of corn and cut corn off of cobs with a sharp knife. Give cobs to chickens and ducks. They love corn day! Give the outer leaves to the goats. They love them! Save the corn silk in a paper bag for healing up urinary tract infections. Just make into tea with a handful of cranberries, juniper berries and honey.

2. Fill warm jars with corn to half an inch from the rim. Add 1/2 a teaspoon of sea salt to pints, 1 teaspoon to quarts. Fill jars to 1/2 an inch from rim with a kettle of hot water. Wipe off rim and put on lid.

3. Fill the pressure canner with three inches of water. Put jars in canner. Attach lid. (Note: the new pressure canners are inexpensive and not our great-grandma's pressure canners. They do not blow up! There is no fear using one!) Turn on high and when the shaker starts shakin' and it sounds like you ought to be belly dancing, start timing. 55 minutes for pints, 85 minutes for quarts. For high altitude canning, always use all the weights. For the rest of the world use 10 pounds of pressure.

A burlap bag 2/3 full made 10 pints of corn and 3 quarts of corn. I need thirty jars to get through winter (we love corn) so I'll need another bag!

Perfect Pickled Eggs

The first time we ate a pickled egg was at Nancy's house a few years ago. She put out a platter of olives, crackers, chutney, and pickled eggs to enjoy with our glasses of wine out on the deck in the waning sunlight. The eggs were a royal purple with brightly colored yolks. We hesitated, and then tried one. Then we promptly ate all of the pickled eggs and asked for more.

Such a surprise they were, and so delicious! So, last year I made my own. You make them with beets so that the glorious color transfers to the plain white eggs. I put up several quarts of pickled eggs and beets. We picked out all the eggs and wasted most of the pickled beets. So this year I did mostly eggs with a much smaller amount of beets, enough for one salad, but enough to turn our beautiful eggs into works of art.

Pickled Eggs and Beets

Hard boil as many eggs as you see fit.

In clean pint jars layer sliced or chopped beets (I do not even peel them, just scrub them up.) with peeled boiled eggs to an inch from the top.

Add a tablespoon of brown sugar, a teaspoon of pumpkin pie spice, and a half teaspoon of salt. Fill half way with water, and the rest of the way (leaving a half inch head space) with vinegar (white or apple cider). Make sure the rim is clean and replace lid.

Place jars in a pot of boiling water with water just covering lids. Bring back to boil and process for 30 minutes. Add one more minute per 1000 feet above sea level. I just round up to 7000 feet, so I boil the jars for 37 minutes. Remove from water and cool on counter until you hear the harmonious sound of popping jars preserving your bounty for winter snacks!

Ginger Spiced Apple Sauce and Trees

Thousands of apples covered the ground and still many hung from the branches. Nipped by the early hail storm, small for the year, invisible to the bugs, they were small, pocked, and perfect. Piles went in to a bag for apple sauce, a pile of bruised ones for the chickens, and a pile for Nancy (who is my fellow lover of canning). Even with all those pounds of apples taken, it looked like the apples replenished themselves before our very eyes, for no spaces on the ground or on the branches were seen. The amount of apples this year was astonishing.

We picked out two year old trees; ones the girl at the nursery said might actually produce an apple or two for us this year. Very exciting! Two apples and a plum tree set off in the back of the truck for new lands, our back yard. We planted them with an existing, much rejected apple tree in the back yard, which was not much bigger. The large apple tree next door laughed. But I shall have the last laugh, I thought, as I envisioned myself picking luscious apples off of the new trees. Savoring the fruit of our hands... and prayers. God forgot to send me a memo about watering. For the first few months I watched and if it rained (which wasn't much) I didn't water. If it didn't, I would lug out a five gallon container of water and give each tree a nice drink...like once a week. It must have been a tease for them once farmer's markets started for our trees did not get the proper water they should have and the drought didn't help the cute little mini forest either. They are alas still standing and trying not to be dead. Not sure what the mysterious holes at their base are either, I hope not voles. So, here with the ground in snow and Christmas presents to wrap, my mind wanders to next year's garden and orchard, as it does every year upon year; next year will be the best year ever!

All those apples were from my Great-Aunt Donna's yard. She is an amazing grower, a Master Gardener, 85 years old, spry as they come and I hope future generations will speak of me the way I speak of her and will come to my yard to gather piles of apples.

GINGER SPICED APPLE SAUCE:

You don't even need a recipe for this. You cannot mess it up. Throw all the apples in the pan (I do not peel them, just take out the core) and add a bit of apple juice to keep it from sticking to the bottom before the natural juices come out, just a big splash now, not too much. You don't have to add sugar, apples are quite sweet, but I do fancy a little honey or brown sugar in mine. Cook this down over medium heat until you are able to put an immersion blender in and get it nice and thick and a little chunky. (My immersion blender will have to be replaced with a food mill for our homestead) Add in a big spoonful of pumpkin pie spice and about half of that spoon of powdered ginger. Taste and adjust flavors. A pinch of salt wouldn't hurt. You can eat the sauce just like this or you might like to can it. Ladle into pint jars leaving ½ inch head space, and replace the lid (I cheat and only rinse the jars and lids in really hot water) and boil in a pot of water that covers the jars for 17 minutes at our altitude. (10 minutes for sea level and add one minute per 1000 feet of altitude.) Yum. Not too late to go get some apples and make this delicious sauce!

Gin and Jelly (sounds like a rap song!)

Chokecherries by themselves are rather tart and cannot be eaten plain, however if you boil them with water then the juice can be turned into all sorts of delights!   Here are a few recipes for chokecherries to save the delightful taste of summer.

CHOKECHERRY GIN:

Fill a half gallon canning jar with chokecherries

Add 3 cups of sugar (organic and raw preferably)

Fill jar with gin.

Let sit for at least two months. Shake daily for the first week to dissolve sugar.

I don't strain it until the liquid is below the fruit. The color becomes a deep purple.

My friend, Sandy, adds more sugar half way through the waiting time and hers is quite spectacular. I may do the same this year. A nip of this concoction during the holidays or on a cold evening in front of the fire is very satisfying and very tasty. Incredibly smooth and easy to drink, do keep in mind it is straight gin! Make mixed drinks with it as well. The gorgeous, festive color lends itself to fine holiday gifts. Just pour into a decorative jar and arrange a ribbon about its neck.

CHOKECHERRY JELLY:

This, my dear friends, is the first time that my chokecherry jelly has set completely! I have made a good deal of chokecherry syrup over the years unintentionally. (Which is quite delicious blended with maple syrup and poured over waffles.) My friend, Liza, brought me a magazine and in it was a recipe for chokecherry jelly which used two packets of liquid pectin rather than one as I had been doing. And it worked!

This recipe is a variation of the one from the Fall 2014 Capper's Farmer magazine.

Place 1 quart of chokecherries in a saucepan and cover with about two inches of water. Boil until the color is lovely and the seeds are all showing through the skin. Strain liquid.

Put 3 cups of juice in pan.

Add 6 1/2 cups of sugar (organic and raw preferably) and 1/2 teaspoon of vanilla sea salt (optional).

Bring to rolling boil stirring constantly.

Add two packets of liquid pectin and return to boil. Boil for two minutes.

Take off heat and add a teaspoon of vanilla extract. Pour into half pint and/or 4 ounce jars leaving ½ inch head space. Clean rim and replace lids. Boil in large pan with water covering jars for 6 minutes. 12 minutes if you are in my neck of the woods.

Mmm...Chokecherry jelly and peanut butter sandwiches, chokecherry jelly on biscuits, on toast, in oatmeal, in salad dressing, in barbeque sauce, in....

Making and Canning Juice

We were gifted three boxes of apples, a windfall from our friends' tree. After putting up eight jars of sliced apples, nine jars of applesauce, and drying a load of apples, I still had a box and a half. Doug and I go through a fair amount of juice and organic juice is not cheap y'all. Here's how to make delicious juices from windfalls, purchased boxes of fruit, and/or frozen fruit to keep all winter. It's ridiculously easy.

Load up a large pot 2/3 full of fruit. I sliced apples in half (I did not even bother to core them, I just made sure they didn't have bugs in them!) and did one batch of just apple. The second batch I threw in the contents of the partial bags of frozen fruit in the freezer. Cranberries, raspberries, and a few strawberries joined the mix, adding their own festive color. A couple of cinnamon sticks and a cup of brown sugar for fun went in as well. My favorite was a pot of pears with great swirls of honey mixed in. This juice was the best of all.

Fill the pot to a few inches from the top with water and boil lightly for two hours. Pour into clean quart jars leaving ½ inch head space, wipe the rims off, replace the lids and place in a large pot with water covering the jars. Boil for 10 minutes. Add 1 minute per 1000 feet above sea level. I boiled for 17 minutes.

Once the lids seal, mark them and place them in the pantry. They are good for at least two years and you didn't waste a single fruit!

Canning Before Summer (beans please!)

Now's the time for canning! It is cold outdoors and the stove practically calls for the steam from a pressure cooker to ease the dry air. Pity the tomatoes in the garden aren't done....oh wait, the ground is covered in snow, no tomatoes. There is plenty of canning to do, however, and as farm girls we'd be wise to get some of it done. Stews and soups can be canned right now. They become leftovers for next fall when time runs short and dinner wants to be served! What I love to have canned are beans. I made the error of canning quarts and pints galore of pinto, black, kidney, and Anasazi beans in the same hot kitchen as the corn, green beans, and other items being stocked in the root cellar. I needed them, so I suppose it wasn't a waste. But it sure was hot and it took up valuable summer vegetable canning time. I am down to my last two jars of kidney beans (apparently our last choice for beans) and now I realize that this is the time to can beans! I could get several quarts and pints put up and they will take me through to the cooler days of autumn.

I love having canned beans at the ready. I have good intentions but often I forget that I teach classes a few evenings a week and things come up and the two to three hour boil on the stove for beans doesn't always transpire. Besides being settled into a toxic can in the store for God knows how long, organic beans are expensive and the cute fifteen ounces seems ridiculous after you turn a bag of organic beans into quarts of beans! For the very same price of a can of beans one can get a bag of organic beans. More money left over for seed potatoes and new grandbaby clothes!

You just need one snow day to get it all done; it is so easy. As vegetarians, beans are a staple in this house. As a New Mexican food junkie, pinto beans and Anasazi beans are quite necessary. White beans are a mouthwatering addition to Italian soups and homemade pastas. Sweet, smoky baked beans and hot crisp bread....ok, I am making myself hungry, on to the lesson!

(Adapted from the Ball Blue Book Guide to Preserving....changed for our altitude)

2 1/4 pounds of dried beans is the suspected measurement to make one quart but I always come up a little short or have too much

for exactly even pints or quarts. Anything that doesn't fill a jar gets turned into tonight's supper.

Soak by covering beans with a few inches of water, bring to boil for a few minutes then turn off heat and let sit for an hour or so. Drain, rinse.

Put beans back in pot and cover with a few inches of cold water and bring to boil. Boil for about 30 minutes.

Pack hot beans and liquid (high altitude means you will need a little extra water than what is in the pot) into prepared canning jars leaving one inch head space. Run a knife around the sides to get rid of excess air bubbles. One could, if they were so inclined, slide in a sprig or rosemary, a bit of sage, or a pinch of chipotle powder. Add 1 teaspoon of sea salt to quarts and 1/2 teaspoon of sea salt to pints.

When the beans are ready to go, place jars in large pressure cooker filled with three inches of water (now, don't be afraid; the new pressure cookers do not explode!), replace lid. In high altitude, use 15 pounds of pressure and when the top starts a tickin' (it sounds like a good Latin music vibe, start shaking your hips), time it for 1 hour and 22 minutes for pints or 1 hour 37 minutes for quarts.

Let that puppy cool down before opening the lid. Let all steam escape and warm up your house. Place jars on counter to cool and listen to the soothing 'pop, pop' of the lids while visions of Huevos Rancheros, White bean and Sage soup, and Cajun Red beans and Rice dance through your head.

I just label the lid with a sharpie with what I put in them and the date. They are good for a year at least. You'll eat them up much faster though!

Freezing

For when you don't have time to can or if you prefer the flavor.

Shelling and Freezing Peas

(an all-day venture, bring friends!)

My entire to-do list was shot yesterday. The day went a bit like this, Pat came over while waiting for her car to be fixed and we spent two hours shelling peas. Then we went to lunch and she went home. I put Doug to work. We spent four more hours shelling peas until the box was gone! Fingers stained black and green, tired shoulder muscles, and two gallon sized freezer bags of peas was our reward.

I had big plans this year that I would grow everything we ate fresh and preserved this summer. Peas were a learning lesson. I grew three five gallon buckets of them and knew pretty quickly I would be short, so I started some in the garden as well. But in the end I will have enough to eat fresh for a few meals. I went to my favorite farm to get a large case of peas. Next year I will plant earlier and I will plant 250 feet of pea rows.

Last year we canned several jars of peas and they were very nice to have all winter. I did begin to tire of the mushy consistency, however, so this year I decided to freeze them.

After shelling two tons of peas, throw them in a pot of boiling water. Let come back up to boil and count to sixty. Immediately strain in colander.

Then pour into a prepared pan of ice water and let sit for a minute or so.

I spread the peas out among cookie sheets and stuck them in the freezer while I went to water the gardens. They were not completely frozen when I came back in but they were enough that they wouldn't freeze into one giant block once in bags. That would make things a smidge difficult if you only needed one cup of peas for a recipe!

Shovel into freezer bags and freeze. Enjoy fresh peas come December. Preserving is fun and rewarding and best done with friends!

Year Round Greens

Now in November I had every intention of getting every bed cleaned out properly, covering them with compost then mulch for their long winter's nap. A good kink in my shoulder decided otherwise. It would have been nice to have it all done, but it will surely wait for me, I decided. So, on the bed that we started putting manure on, I noted emerald green from the patch of otherwise browned kale, chard, and collards. Tiny Swiss chard leaves, two inches high were trying with all their might to grow. It certainly was an epiphany for me. If I cover the greens well with loose straw next year, I could be harvesting well into January! That is without the help of a greenhouse, hoop house, or cold frame. An easy way to extend the season.

Since I did not expect any more greens after November, I had been diligently snipping greens and freezing them. No blanching necessary. I have no desire to eat slimy food...ever. All you do is pack sandwich bags with greens, release the air, and zip closed. Put in freezer. The next day it will be frozen solid. Don't let it thaw! Just crush it between your fingers so that the greens are crumbles. When you need greens, crush the ones on top more and sprinkle handfuls into whatever you are cooking. Replace the rest in freezer immediately.

I have been putting greens in all kinds of soups, in omelets, scrambled eggs, on potatoes to be roasted, and in sautés. There are innumerable ways to use greens and the nutrients are especially desired this time of year. The perfect blend of calcium and magnesium to make it bio-available, iron, A, C, E, and K, full of anti-oxidants and cancer killing properties.

Greens are one of the foods that I would have with me if I were trapped on an island...along with margaritas. Is that a food?

What the Freezer Holds

I like to can. I spend a full day once a week all summer and fall, and perhaps more this year, in the hundred plus degree kitchen (we are making an outdoor kitchen this year) just to make sure that all winter we have some pretty great vegetable dishes that taste fresh out of the garden...even during snow storms. But some things don't can so well.

Eggplant for instance. Imagine that sucker canned. Soaked in water. Gag. Okay, now imagine it sliced thinly, pulled from the freezer, dredged in fresh egg and cornmeal with lots of spices and baked until crisp. Drool. So, no canning eggplant. Freezing is the only way to go. Simply slice up the eggplant, place pieces on a cookie sheet and freeze. Then transfer frozen slices into a freezer bag labeled.

The freezer is overflowing with tomatoes. I brought tons home with very good intentions of canning yet another dozen or more jars. So into bags they went and were placed in the freezer with intentions to can them...sometime. They are great though. Pop three of them into a crockpot with half a chopped onion, six cloves of garlic, two cups of pinto beans, six cups of water or broth and some taco seasoning. Put that baby on high for six hours and enjoy the world's easiest and mouthwatering dinner. They simply dissolve into a gorgeous broth.

Mushrooms get frozen around here because mushrooms canned are a tad slimy for our liking. They go from freezer to batter to fried in no time or added to pasta sauce or stew.

Peppers are particularly fun because all you have to do is cut them in half into little boats, take out the seeds, and line them up on a cookie sheet, freeze, and layer into a freezer bag. Enjoy stuffed peppers all winter long. Once you cook them, they collapse a little and absorb the juices from the filling. Since my family doesn't care for stuffed peppers, they are saved for entertaining.

One year, I grilled slices of eggplant, peppers, zucchini, and onions. I chopped them up and placed into sandwich bags. They came out of the freezer as ready-made pizza toppings. We went through them pretty quickly. Last year, out of time, I took all the vegetables off of the grill and placed them into bags. I did not cut them up. They are still in the freezer waiting to become some fabulous dish. But alas, I will probably never defrost them and cut them up. Prepping in the summer may seem like a pain when one is already short on time, but so worth it when it comes to leisurely eating all winter!

Frozen zucchini slices are still sitting in the freezer. Soggy zucchini doesn't appeal to me. I probably should wait until they are fresh again.

Corn can be shucked and four ears can be placed in a gallon freezer bag. Simply take out, throw into boiling water for five minutes, butter and salt and enjoy summertime eating in January.

Lastly, any leftover soups or beans are placed in the freezer for later use. Sometimes we don't get to that big pot of soup (I am still having trouble figuring out how much to cook) in the next week and it morphs into something entirely different in the back of the fridge. The chickens love when that happens. But, if I place it in a freezer bag, mark what it is, and put it in the freezer, I can pop it out, place it in the stock pot, bag and all, and by the time I am ready to make dinner, I just pour it out and heat it up. Homestead fast food.

What I did though was place bags of screwed up food in there. I made beans, way too many beans, and put way too much pepper in them. No one ate them. I couldn't bring myself to waste them so I froze them thinking I could "fix" them on the next meal. Every time I see them in there I turn up my nose. The chickens are about to have a feast coming up soon. I need to clean out the freezer.

The main con is the electricity use. I have an energy saving model but it doesn't do me any good when the electricity goes out. I opened the door to a swimming mess of juices a few weeks ago. Denial is my friend so I just closed the door and walked away. I will probably have to tend to that this week! I don't eat meat so I don't worry about half defrosted green pepper halves harming me. It just irritates me that my ice cream melted.

The freezer can be your friend. One more homesteading helper to preserve that delicious harvest, whether it be out of your garden or from a local farm's. Not having to grocery shop for vegetables mid-winter and the pride of having fed yourself and your family is a pretty great thing!

By the way, I do not blanch many of the above items. They all keep just fine and if I had to take the time to blanch them, they wouldn't ever make it to the freezer!

Dehydrating

Concentrating flavor and letting air do the work for you.

Dehydrating Dinner

I have talked about canning, freezing, and root cellaring. There is another way to preserve food! Dehydrating. It is easy, saves space, concentrates flavors, and who doesn't love a dried cinnamon apricot?

I bought my fancy dehydrator when Doug and I were on our Raw Foodie kick. We used our income tax refund to purchase a Vitamix and the Excalibur dehydrator. Luckily we bought high quality items so that even now they work fabulously. The Excalibur has temperature controls so you can control how quickly or how slowly you want to dehydrate your food. I layer the trays with apples (disappeared in two weeks upon completion), apricots (just finished the bag. I hid it for a while so Doug wouldn't finish them in two weeks as well), and tomatoes. The finished product slides into zip lock bags and sits in the basement.

The first year that I dehydrated food to put up for winter, I only processed it to the point where it looks like the ones in the stores. The stores add a preservative. So those juicy looking dried tomatoes quickly molded and the whole batch was ruined. At home I have to dehydrate everything until there is no sign of moisture. You could dehydrate it until moist and eatable now but then you would have to freeze them and that seems counterproductive to me! The apricots are not crispy, just leathery. Same with the apples. The tomatoes are hard, so are the peas, green beans, and carrots that I dehydrated and put in canning jars.

We are able to chew on the leathery fruit for a while as it slowly starts to reconstitute, releases juices, and becomes a satisfying snack. The tomatoes I pour boiling water over and let sit until I am able to snip them with scissors into smaller pieces and drop into sauce. The same can be done with the soup vegetables as well as dried mushrooms from the store if you don't grow them (something I'd like to learn). I made the error of throwing the peas, green beans, and carrots in with rice while it was cooking. Sautéed it all together with soy sauce and egg to make a stir fry. We all bit into it, made a face. They were still pretty hard. I prepare the dried vegetables first before adding them to meals now! You can add the water you soaked them in to stock or sauces. Particularly the mushroom broth, very rich and tasty. You can bring the vegetables to a boil for five to ten minutes to reconstitute as well.

I thought last year, as I am trying to do things without electricity more, that I would sun dry all these things. I placed my large folding rack for laundry on the hot back porch and balanced the trays from the dehydrator between the rungs. An hour later they looked great until closer inspection when I noticed all of the ants. I read that if one sprinkles cinnamon around the trays the ants will stay off. Ants love cinnamon at my house, apparently. I brought everything back in and finished it in the dehydrator. But I tell you what, the cinnamon apricots were my favorite! Maybe covering the fruit and vegetables with cheesecloth next time?

This year I would like to dehydrate onions. I buy a tremendous amount of dried, minced onion because I love the flavor in food. I sat there while opening the bag thinking, "I could do this!" Isn't that how homesteading starts? Look at something that you always buy or always use and think, "I could do this!"

For fruit, just slice in half, core or remove pit, and dip in lemon juice before lying in single layers on racks. For tomatoes, just cut in half and place cut side down. Romas work best for this. For other vegetables, just slice and lay on racks. Dehydrate until moisture is gone. For delicious Roma tomatoes that are not too dry, dehydrate until still a bit plump but mostly shriveled and pack into canning jars. Top with olive oil and store in refrigerator.

I hope you are planning on preserving lots of food this year. In these uncertain times it sure feels good to have a full larder and dehydrating can help bolster your stores!

Root Cellar

Not many of us have a proper root cellar anymore but we like to call the pantry and basement the root cellar.

What the Pantry Holds

Putting up food is not just a prepper ideal for potential zombie attacks, nor is it folly or old fashioned. It is smart. One good snow storm or emergency could leave you home bound. One lost job or identity theft could keep you from spending money. Having a house stocked with food is important and takes away a lot of worry and fear.

In a pinch, you could blend together baking powder, oil, flour, salt, and water to make fluffy biscuits for breakfast or guests. Then use jam from the root cellar and you have a fabulous treat. You can make bread from just salt, yeast, flour, and water. You can make a lot of delicious meals more filling with cooked farro, barley, couscous, or rice. Dried beans are at the ready to simmer all day to enjoy on a cold winter's night with some warm bread.

Organic bulk grains, nuts, seeds, beans, legumes, and flours are fairly inexpensive and can make several meals complete. I store mine in canning jars so that I can see what I have. Otherwise they become mountains of staples in the pie safe that I forget I had. One positive thing about closing my retail front was reclaiming one of my display pieces. It is a sixty plus year old hardware shelving unit with several cubbies. I love the look of it, the numbered spaces, and the vintage appeal it lends to my kitchen. It is becoming a wine rack/staples case. Filled with canning jars of nuts, beans, and different grains and flours, and of course, wine, it will lend an easy air to cooking in my kitchen this winter.

Look for split peas, lentils, pinto beans, white navy beans, rice, barley, couscous, cornmeal, walnuts, pine nuts, anything you enjoy, and fill the canning jars with them. Display. They look great out and make cooking dinner more inspiring.

Hibernation for the Pressure Canner (and the farmer)

524.   Final count of canned items.   The last was this week's potatoes. Twenty jars of ready to cook potatoes joined the ranks of winter and spring food. The canners are going into hibernation now. Hurray! As much as I enjoy the salsa dancing sound of the pressure cooker, I am ready to just settle down and eat my way through the root cellar.

I planned out early how much I needed to can of each thing. Rough estimates for sure. Let's see, green beans once a week until May...tomatoes and sauce twice a week...had too much of this last year left over....not enough of that. A hopeful sketch emerged and the root cellar checklist I made will head downstairs on a clipboard. I'll be even more efficient next year.

The potatoes are in their wire crates. The butternut squash is too. The onions are in a box. The corn is drying. The carrots are in a five gallon bucket emerged in slightly damp sand. There is a large bag of sugar, a fifty pound bag of flour on order, buckets of whole grains to grind. There is the surrounding air of deep satisfaction and peace.

Part 5 (Make Your Own)

Generally speaking, if you can buy it, you can make it.)

Make Your Own Soap!

Alright, let's make soap! It is easy, you can make it however you like, and you will never buy another bar of drying, chemical laden soap again!

First, gather your ingredients. You can buy these items online at places like Brambleberry or Essential Depot but I like to support local business so I head down to Buckley's Homestead Supply in Old Colorado City and pick up what I am missing.

You will need a digital scale to measure your ingredients. Place the digital scale in a plastic freezer bag to protect it. When dealing with lye use safety glasses and rubber gloves. But don't be overly scared of it to the point that you scare yourself out of using it. I have licked my finger thinking I had coconut oil on it, rubbed my face, dropped it on my bare foot....a bit of good lotion, salve, or lavender essential oil and a washing gets the sting out really quick. You will also need a plastic pitcher, a plastic spoon, a plastic mixing bowl, and a plastic spatula (see the pattern here?). I get mine from the dollar store and only use them for soap making. You will also need a red solo cup, a measuring cup, and a soup pot. Only the things that touch lye need to remain solely for soap. My soup pot and measuring cups stay in the kitchen. You will need an immersion blender and a laser thermometer as well.

You can purchase molds or you can chop the top off of a paper milk carton and use that.

You will need 16 oz. of liquid. I use goat's milk. I have also used half goat's milk and half wine and one time I did half goat's milk and half coffee. That was a great bar of soap! You could use beer, water, or store bought milk. How about beet juice for the color or green tea? Just don't use anything acidic like orange juice or pineapple juice as the lye will react to it.

7.4 oz. of lye. Pour this into the plastic cup when measuring it on the scale and simply rinse out afterwards.

16 oz. of olive oil

16 oz. of coconut oil

16 oz. of palm oil (I am not crazy about using palm oil but it is what makes the soap hard. One day I'll learn to make lard soap and then we won't need the palm oil.)

2 oz. of castor oil (This is what makes it sudsy.)

2 oz. of essential oil. Now don't get crazy and get 2 ounces of cinnamon or something, you don't want the soap to be super hot! Try vanilla, or lavender, rose, maybe orange and peppermint, a combination of oils, or pine for Christmas, or maybe just coffee scented if you used coffee as your liquid and skip the essential oils! I am not a proponent of multi-marketing oils, just find a good essential oil at the local health store at an affordable price and use it. Don't use fragrances!

1. Now that we have everything assembled let's get started! Place the liquid in the plastic pitcher and put the plastic spoon in it. Put your glasses and gloves on and slowly pour the lye into the cup. Now put the laser thermometer in your apron pocket and take the pitcher and the lye outside. Make sure there are no chickens around to tip the thing over or curious dog noses! Slowly pour the lye into the liquid while stirring. It will get really hot, about 175 degrees and will change color. We have this outside so we don't asphyxiate folks in the house. Outside it will cool faster as well.

2. Back inside measure all oils, except the essential oils, those go in at the end of the process, and place in a pot. Warm on a wood cook stove (or regular stove) until the oils have just melted.

3. Taking temperatures. Now here is where we get our workout. Check the temperature of the oils. You can alter the temps by sticking it in the snow or fridge or reheating it. The oils will cool down faster than the lye. Once the lye cools down there is no reheating it so this is the point that you have to be rather diligent about watching temps. The goal is to get the oil and the lye to 105

degrees at precisely the same time. There can be a one degree temperature difference. But ideally, 105. Bring lye in when it is 120 degrees to slow it down while you work on the oil temperature.

4. Prepare the bowl, set up the immersion blender, have the tops off the essential oils ready to pour in all at once and have some paper towel on hand. Put gloves and glasses on. When the oil and the lye are ready, pour the oil into the bowl, and then slowly pour the lye mixture in. Keep the immersion blender below the liquid line or you will spray soap everywhere! Blend until the mixture starts to feel like pudding. When you can swirl the blender (turned off) over the top of the mixture and it makes swirly lines that is called tracing. Add essential oils, and any additions for exfoliation (oatmeal, coffee grounds, poppy seeds...) and continue to blend until almost cake batter consistency then pour into mold.

5. Place a piece of cardboard over mold and wrap in a towel. Leave for 24 hours. After 24 hours peel back paper or take out of mold and slice with a kitchen knife into desired size. I generally like one inch thick pieces of soap. Place small side down on dresser and let cure for four weeks. Wrap and give as gifts or store in a zip lock bag to retain scent.

Homesteading skills like making soap are fun, save money, and will always come in handy!

Make Your Own Cleaning Products

Spring cleaning time! Did you know that conventional cleaners are very toxic? They can cause issues like asthma and even cancer. They do seep through the skin and are inhaled. They are also very expensive! Not only that, but they are very hard on the environment as they never really go away, they just sit in our waterways. You can save a bundle, and have a really clean, green, and healthy home by making your own cleaning products. And yes, they work every bit as well as conventional.

Dusting Oil - This makes wood look brand new and super shiny. The oil does dissipate.

Combine 3 oz. of olive oil and 1 oz. of lemon juice with 30 drops of lemon essential oil (or orange!) Use an old cloth to apply. Dust as usual. Note: I use pieces of old socks. I just throw the piece into the compost heap and not get oil all over everything in the wash.

Window Cleaner - Make sure you clean windows when the sun is behind the clouds or you will get streaks!

Combine 8 oz. of water and 8 oz. of white vinegar with 10 drops of lime essential oil into a spray bottle.

All-purpose Cleaner - Add water to spray bottle first so that it doesn't bubble over and all the soap is lost!

Combine 14 oz. of water and 2 oz. of Dr. Bronner's soap with 30 drops of essential oils of your choice. One could also cut up half a bar of homemade soap and put in a large spray bottle and top with water.

Wood/Floor Cleaner -

Combine 4 oz. of almond Castile soap (like Dr. Bronner's), 1 T of almond oil, 10 drops of orange essential oil in a container. Squirt a little bit into a big tub and top with hot water.

Toilet Cleaner -

Toss in baking soda then add vinegar and watch it bubble, bubble. Add a squirt of Dr.Bronner's and use a brush to scrub.

Room Spray -

Combine 3 oz. of witch hazel, 1 oz. of water, and 60 drops of essential oil of your choice in a squirt bottle.

Aromatherapy Choices -

Tea Tree- Anti-bacterial, anti-viral, as good as bleach, kills mold, anti-fungal

Citrus (Lemon, Orange, Tangerine, Grapefruit)- Uplifting

Floral (Lavender, Rose, Jasmine)- Romantic

Peppermint or Spearmint- Uplifting

Cinnamon, pine, cedar, clove, or any of your favorite scents make fabulous cleaning products and room sprays.

We use Dr. Bronner's or other castile soap to clean dishes and laundry. Borax, washing soda, baking soda, and vinegar are powerful artillery in the home cleaning arsenal.

Make Your Own Body Products

Just for fun! It's nice to see that simple things in the kitchen cupboard and nature can provide everything we need if we wanted or needed to use it. These are truly the cleanest body products around!

Shampoo:

From the cupboard- Baking soda. Put a little in your hand and make a paste with water. Only wash the scalp. Rinse. Follow with homemade conditioner.

From the field- Yucca roots or Lamb's quarters roots boiled will release saponin which is essentially soap! It won't lather but it will clean.

Conditioner:

From the cupboard- Apple cider vinegar. (Use before you shave your legs. Just sayin'.) The smell does not linger. Pour over hair and rinse. Super shiny hair will ensue.

From the field- Rosemary tea for dark hair, chamomile tea for blonde hair. (Make tea by pouring 1 cup of boiling water over 1-2 teaspoons of herbs.)

Soap:

From the cupboard- Olive oil was used in centuries past as a cleanser. Also doubles as moisturizer!

From the field- A sponge bath of rose, lavender, and yucca root or lambs quarters tea will be quite refreshing.

Toothpaste:

From the cupboard- Baking soda. Whitens, cleans, disinfects.

From the field- A sage leaf. I use this when I feel like I have a bit of "coffee breath" as I run out the door. I keep a pot of it on the front porch. Simply run the leaf around your teeth and tongue and receive instant fresh breath and clean teeth.

You can get your toothbrush in a pinch from the field as well. Pioneers often used the root of the Mallow plant.

Mouthwash:

From the cupboard- A bit of apple cider vinegar.

From the field- Chew on parsley, sage, or peppermint.

Deodorant:

From the cupboard- 1/2 teaspoon of sea salt dissolved in a cup of water. Spray or apply with cotton ball.

From the field- Crushed mint leaves, or rose water.

Body Scrub:

From the cupboard- Sugar or Salt blended with a little olive oil.

From the field- Straight mud! It's actually quite lovely.

How to make rose water two ways:

Steam distillation (this is how you make any flower essences)- Place a brick or rock in the center of a large pot and set a bowl on top of stone. Surround the stone with rose petals then pour a few inches of water over flowers. Replace lid to pot and simmer water. The water that condenses on the lid and drips into the bowl is your flower essence. Pour this into a spray bottle and add more water or witch hazel.

Infusion- Pour two cups of boiling water over a cup of rose petals and let steep for 30 minutes. Pour into spray bottle. Add a little witch hazel if desired.

Use the rose water to refresh skin and brighten mood. Will keep in the refrigerator for about 3-5 days.

Make Your Own Candles

Candle making is a true farm girl skill. We go through a lot of candles here, to make the house smell nice and to read by, so sometimes it is nice to supplement with ones I have made. I think various molds would be fun to try, tapers and tea candles and such, but without all of the fun trimmings and trappings of fancy candle making, I have resorted to using coffee cups. Or canning jars. You can find wax and wicks at homesteading stores or online. I purchased a giant bag of organic soy wax and the wicks that I thought would work. (I really had no idea, I simply guessed!)

I have a separate pan and measuring cup when dealing with wax. Once or twice you can get all the wax out and scrub it up nice, but we simply make too many lotions, salves, and now candles to have to worry about it. So, these instruments are specifically for wax. They ain't pretty, but they get the job done. Pour wax to the top of the measuring cup and heat water to boiling. As the wax melts, stir it with a chop stick and add more wax until the finished product is about 2 cups. Do not add any water or oils, just straight wax.

Ahh, my old nemesis, the wick. It insists upon releasing its grip, and running amuck as soon as I pour the wax in. It is truly a test of my patience. I have found a few tricks. Use a good glue, and glue the bottom of the wick to the bottom of the coffee cup. Press down on the metal part with a chopstick. The longer you leave it, the less likely it will dislodge and become a horizontal wick!

Twist the wick (carefully) around the chopstick to hold it in place.

When the wax looks completely melted, give it a stir again.

Pour into containers.

A Note on Scents: Now is the time to add fragrance or essential oils to your product. You will add them into the coffee cup or the wax, your choice. Funny story about the oils. I wanted all natural scents wafting through my house. So, I used about 60 drops of essential oil and...nothing. Not strong enough. I used an ounce of essential oil. Emily casually walked in and said, "Your candle is on fire." I said, "Oh good! I can smell the pine essential oil from here!"

She instructed me to go see the candle and sure enough, the whole thing was on fire with my hutch not far behind it! Bonfire in the living room! So, I just use enough essential oil to cover the metal ring at the bottom of the wick, but alas it doesn't really emit much scent. So, I broke down and bought fragrance oils. I can tell people how bad they are all I want, but at the end of the day at Walmart when I am picking up smelly candles....Well, I may as well buy the fragrance oil and try to save a few bucks. I poured an ounce of oil into the coffee cups, and they aren't bad but they aren't like Yankee Candle either, so I am not sure what the trick is. Most people like softly scented or scent free candles anyway! Fragrance oils are endocrine disruptors so if you have thyroid problems, you may want to opt for essential oils.

Make Your Own Herbal Medicines

Would you like to improve your health and not have to go to the doctor every time you get sick or injured? Would you like to take the fear out of becoming ill? Would you like to not worry about side effects ever again? This sounds like an infomercial. But, these are not empty promises. Once you start working with herbs, it is hard to go back to medicines with warnings that are scarier than a horror movie. Even the over the counter drugs are deadly.

Many folks have tried herbal supplements from the store with varying degrees of success. "I have tried black cohosh, it didn't work." or "I tried Gingko but it gave me paralysis in my right leg." The biggest part of my job is not making medicines, but educating. The herbs in the store are half dead, folks. If you shove three leaves of something with a bunch of additives into a pill, it isn't going to work, or at least not to its full potential. How old are those herbs? How long have they been sitting on the shelf? And herbs cannot hurt you. The herbs that are used to make medicines cannot hurt you.

Tinctures in the health food store are made of 20% extract and 80% glycerin and water. Why? Because one can get a lot more product from one vat of extract and it improves the taste. It also lessens the benefit. Why waste your time and money? When people try my medicines for the first time, they are amazed. Just last week a gentleman bought the Diabetes medicine from me, a bit skeptical, but what the heck he says, and it lowered his numbers in twenty minutes. The reason is because I don't cut mine with anything. I brew these things up to their full potential. Put them in the full moon for maximum frequency change (just like female cycles, ocean waves, biodynamic farming, the moon changes the frequency of the medicines to match our bodies) and I baby the herbs before they started their job. Each batch is hand made. And there is no "herbs take two weeks to start working in the body" here. Same day. I would also like to see you all empowered and whipping up remedies for your friends and family and helping to change the idea that herbs are not as strong as pharmaceutical medicines. Not true.

The other thing we have to fight against is myths surrounding herbs. Herbs are very safe, folks. I am not going to encourage you to wild craft hemlock or poisonous mushrooms. You will start out by purchasing herbs from a reputable herb grower like Mountain Rose Herbs and they will not sell you something poisonous. Neither will a reputable herbalist. We have no reason to poison people! So, now that we have established that Gingko does not cause paralysis, (I swear, if a person even stubs their toe while taking an herb, they blame the plant. Herbs do not harm. They are God's medicine made specifically for your body. The pharmaceuticals were not. They are only in existence for profit.) let's learn how to make some medicines.

Infusion- An infusion is tea. A nice cup of tea. The recipe for this is 1 teaspoon of dried herbs to 1 cup of boiling water and let brew for 4 minutes.

Infusions are typically made from herbs that are easy to brew. A thick bark or root would need to be boiled longer, about forty minutes should you need to do so. Mint leaves, chamomile, and a thin slice of ginger would get rid of heartburn in minutes. Catnip, chamomile, and skullcap would help someone relax enough to sleep. St. John's Wort, borage, and rose petals will help stop a panic attack but also stop the blues. You could blend herbs and use 1 or 2 (I like mine a little stronger) teaspoons in a tea strainer to make the tea or just use single herbs like lemon verbena or thin shavings of willow bark.

Extract- An extract is herbs that have had their medicinal benefits extracted in alcohol. Have you ever made a plum cordial or chokecherry liqueur? Same concept. The alcohol takes on the flavors and medicinal benefits of the plants that are sitting in the booze. Place 1 part plants (dried or fresh) and 4 parts alcohol (not Everclear! Use Vodka, Gin, Rum, Brandy or the like) in a canning jar. Sit this in the window sill for 3 days. Shake, admire, take pictures, these things are gorgeous! Sit out of the sun (but not necessarily in the dark). Then on the full moon put it back in the window sill for three days. Store on a shelf or in a cupboard. Letting it brew for 4 weeks is great. It is ready after 2. A dosage is 1/2 teaspoon for tonics (brain stimulants, energy, heart tonics, daily herbals...) and 1 teaspoon for sleep medicines, mild pain, etc., and upwards of a tablespoon for severe pain. You don't have to worry about overdosing and even small children can take this, just halve their dosage.

Syrup- One could make syrup out of lots of things but let's make a syrup from honey. Put 1 part dried herbs to 2 parts honey in a sauce pan and heat over medium-low heat for twenty minutes shaking pan regularly to mix and keep from burning. When this is done you will see that the herbs are drenched in honey and softened, the color of the honey may have changed, and you can smell the herbs. Strain. Now, to make it a syrup, just cut it with a little apple cider vinegar or brandy. Or leave it the way it is and put in tea.

You have the ability to heal up your own self and family with the help of medicines that have been around before humans! Have faith in what nature has provided. We have seen broken bones heal in two weeks, helped get rid of staph infections in one day, helped keep cancer at bay. Are you interested in becoming an herbalist? I have a school for those of you that want to take this further. Correspondence courses are available. But, in the meantime, for all of us, we can simply make a nice cup of tea, an extract, or a syrup with great ease and effectiveness. www.WhiteWolfHerbs.com

Make Your Own Gifts

Gifts from the heart. From your homestead. Made by the work of your hands. Or something you devised from the nearest craft store. A letter. Let us all strive this year to give each other things of real worth. Nothing that needs to be dusted or that may end up in a landfill. Something that touches our hearts, or souls, or our tummies, or that just makes us smile. Here are some ideas for homemade gifts and a recipe for the best lip balm you will ever try.

1. Use rough yarn, or leftover scraps of yarn to whip up little kitchen wash rags and a pot holder.

2. Anything you canned this year, or if you didn't can this year, it won't take long to cook up some jelly! A beautiful jar of beets, applesauce, or strawberry jam is always a delight to receive.

3. Infused alcohol: place vodka, rum, brandy or other hard liquor in a pretty bottle and drop in vanilla beans and a little brown sugar, or raspberries, hazelnuts and honey, or lemons and sugar, or cinnamon sticks and maple syrup. The combinations are unending, the aperitif unparalleled.

4. Homemade laundry soap.

5. Candles, made by you or not, candles are always nice to have in any lifestyle!

6. A pretty tea cup with your favorite blend of tea and a tea ball.

7. Homemade cookies, fudge, any delight from the kitchen that the recipient may not have had time to make this year.

8. Your prized recipe with a few of the ingredients.

9. A letter telling the person how much they mean to you.

10. Cover half a styrofoam ball with leftover fabric and glue into old teacup flat side down to make a charming pin cushion. Glue cup onto saucer.

11. Seeds and instructions. Your saved seeds even better!

12. Infused honey.

13. The best lip balm: In a double boiler (I put the ingredients into a glass measuring cup inside a saucepan of water) you will need 2 and a half ounces of olive oil, almond, grapeseed, or apricot kernel oil. Add to that 1 oz of shea butter, and 1 oz of chopped up beeswax. While that is melting prepare the lip balm containers (available online, I get mine at http://mountainroseherbs.com). Drop 3 drops of essential oil into each container (spearmint, orange, lemon, or vanilla all make yummy lip balms). When wax mixture has thoroughly melted and you have stirred it with a chopstick several times in the process, pour into each container with great patience. It's quick and kind of messy and worth it. For you will have 20-22 fabulous lip balms in your possession made by you.

The Simplest Gifts

Christmas Eve was upon us again. We gathered around the kitchen table excitedly finishing our supper with Christmas music dancing through the house. Christmas was my mother's favorite time of year and even though the stress of finances was on them, my parents enjoyed the season. Our beautiful tree glistened with old ornaments, funky child-made ornaments, and lights. The same angel that always looked down, did so from her perch that year from the top of the tree. Our stockings were hung, on the wall, so it seems, no fireplace was there. The three of us giggling and trying very hard to be good looked out into the dark December sky and saw a red light flying by. Heidi yelled, "Rudolph is coming, hurry!" (Perhaps it was a plane, but it being Rudolph was much more likely being Christmas Eve and all.) We went to bed a wee earlier than usual and stayed awake for what seemed forever with sounds of Mahalia Jackson's, "Go Tell it on the Mountain" and the Andy William's Christmas album singing us to sleep.

Santa must have fallen on rough times as well that year because he brought a toy for us to share. But we were so delighted with the community castle and a "My Little Pony" for each of us. We played and danced and opened our stockings and ate the chocolate and smiled. (Even now, you must eat the chocolate immediately before the dog gets into the stocking and does it for you.) I don't remember this part, but the tree was rather bare that year, my parents were concerned that we would be unhappy with our small gifts.

There was a tea set under the tree from my Grandma and Grandpa. Miniature, real china tea cups with a single sweet rosebud on each with saucers, and a real teapot with the same pink roses. It delighted me so. My mother found invitations that said the "Tuesday Tea Party" and I was allowed to choose a few girls to come to my house after school and have tea with real sugar cubes and little snacks. It was a delight I will not soon forget.

There were not many other gifts but I do remember one. One that would change the course of my life forever. A simple spiral notebook. I can imagine how my parents would have fretted over such simple gifts and our reaction to them as our peers were receiving tape players and Madonna-esqe clothing. "You can write some stories in it," my mother said. I took that as a personal invitation, as if I was not able to write before. I quickly filled the spiral with short stories and poems. I gave them to my fifth grade teacher, Mrs. Cook, to read and she told me to call her when I became an author. An author? I never thought that was an option!

Through teenage turmoil and growing pains, I filled journals and spirals with thousands of poems and thoughts. The notebooks shaped me. As I became a young woman I outlined my dreams of the future in poetical prose. My journal in my twenties was my therapist, hearing every thought and making sense of the jumble and stressors in my mind. It fueled me to start school to be an English teacher (though that was short lived because of finances), but I continued to write.

I have now written cookbooks, a textbook to use in my Certified Herbalist Courses, and was the writer for the "Ask the Herbalist" column in the paper as well as the food and wine writer for another local paper. And now I can write this. All because of a spiral notebook.

What a simple spiral can do in a child's life. My son has filled several with adorable stories and now fills them with music lyrics. So, this Christmas, instead of the newest video game or (gasp) cash (that they will spend on junk food at the gas station, guaranteed!) maybe a beautiful journal with nice pens, or drawing paper and oil pastels, or a beginning knitting or crocheting book and needles and fabulous yarn and a bit of your time, or an apron with wooden spoons and a cookbook. Most adults might enjoy these things too!

Give simply, and see what your gift will become.

Make Your Own Fingerless Gloves

It is Emily's birthday Thursday and I wanted to crochet her something along with a regular gift. I couldn't decide what. Since we girls all crochet, we have a bunch of scarves, hats, and gifts from others. I thought about leg warmers or boot cuffs then I looked down at my own hands. My good friend, Lisa, knitted me some fingerless gloves to keep my hands warm while I type in the early morning chill. They are great. I love them! So, I thought I would make Mims some too.

Thicker yarn comes together quickly but produces a more bulky (but possibly warmer) glove, and thinner yarn takes forever (my patience is staggering) so I used a medium thick yarn in a lovely coral color. I used a crochet hook that looked like the right hole size for the job, not too big, not too small. As you may notice, I wing a lot of stuff. And really, you can't mess it up. You can always pull it out. But have fun choosing the color and feel of your yarn and find a hook that holds that yarn easily and feels good in your hand. This is unconventional information. If the gals at knitting club heard me say this I would certainly get a tisk, tisk.

Chain 14. Turn. Double crochet in the third hole and continue across. (Should have 12)

Turn. Chain 3. Triple crochet in all the holes across. (making sure you have 12)

Continue for 7 rows. (total of 9) Or test it by placing your hand on the square and seeing if when folded that it covers both sides of your hand, not including the thumb.

Slip crochet hook into top hole, grab yarn with hook, and pull through. Continue down the row 5 holes.

Chain 3. Triple crochet in next seven holes to end. Turn.

Chain 3. Triple crochet two more rows. (Total of 3) Knot.

Fold piece together and sew up with yarn, folding the thumb to meet the longer side.

Triple crochet in each of the holes along bottom of glove to create a cuff.

I gave them to Emily early. It only took me one knitting group meeting to make them and she was there so I just handed them to her because I cannot keep secrets, particularly gifts. She drives my big truck that doesn't open without rolling down the window. She drives every day to take her boyfriend to school and then to work. I figured these would be a cute way to keep her hands warm while still being able to finagle the carseat and radio!

Make Your Own School

I was pretty certain I was going to screw up my kids if I did it. I wanted to be a teacher for a while. I majored in English. I love all things academic...except math. But, what if I didn't do it right? The kids had been asking for a few years, off and on, to be homeschooled. I had read in one of my favorite books, Radical Simplicity by Jim Merkel, the recollections of the grandmothers in a village in India where they talked about how once the children went to school they became more immersed in television, consumerism, and a culture that did not reflect that of the previous generations. The children were losing the knowledge of plants and skills and it felt like a great loss to the elders.

I, too, wanted to teach my children how to garden and about herbs. I wanted them to read great books and explore the woods on a weekday and breathe in life. I remembered so clearly being a child sitting in a classroom gazing longingly at the mountains and wishing I were at a nearby park writing poetry and feeding ducks instead of being cooped up learning who knows what that I would eventually forget.

Meanwhile, Andrew was in his first year of high school. Near the end of the school year Andrew had a poor grade in one of his classes and I had emailed the teacher a few times with no response. At the teacher/parent conference I asked her how he was doing.

"Great!" she replied.

"Really?" I retorted. "Then why is he failing?"

"What is his name again?" she asked as she shuffled through her papers.

I could do this better myself, I decided.

I had always done what my son called, Mommy School. Workbooks, library trips, writing club, museums, additional things to help them learn more without seeing it as "education". So, with that I began researching homeschooling. I found a lot of information that I had to glean through. So, here it is in a comprehensive format. It is specifically for Colorado but most places do not have too many variations.

What? Homeschooling is the realization that often times parents are the best teachers and that the wide world around children is often kept from them in favor of a classroom where someone else determines what your child will (or will not) learn. Homeschooling is an important aspect of homesteading as it teaches children self-sufficiency skills, teaches them values, and lessons, as well as providing plenty of time for reading books they wish to read in trees.

Why? Homeschooling is recognizing that information is retained far better when used and learned on one's own accord. It is unfortunate that the standards in schools have gotten out of hand. All children are different, yet the standards are ridiculously rigid. For instance, all children must be able to read by the age of five or they have something wrong with them. The truth is, children can learn to read any time from the ages of four to eight, and making them feel as if something is wrong with them starts the cycle of self-esteem issues early. Children will learn what they need to learn and retain it, much more so if it is on their own terms.

When? Anytime you want. If you work then it is after work or on weekends. Think about how much time is wasted in schools with passing periods, settling in time, time getting to and from school. You can have the equivalent class time in about two hours at home. This also allows homeschoolers to take vacations when others are in school. We used to take the kids to New Mexico or Wyoming or Kansas to see hot air balloons (science), art museums (arts), history and science museums, and on horseback riding adventures. We would study geography by using workbooks and for each country we would research the clothing, art projects, and foods. We went to a fantastic African restaurant in a rough part of town that we would never have tried on our own had we not been looking for it for school. We put cardamom in our coffee and grew seedlings in windows. We read books and participated in events at the library. And a lot of the time was spent playing and building forts in the large open space near our home.

Where? Anywhere you wish. Learning is everywhere and the sooner we figure out that we don't stop learning at eighteen years old or twenty-two from college, the better. We ought to learn our entire lives. Perpetual homeschool!

How? So, you have decided that you would like to give it a go. Really, worst case scenario, you can always send the kids back to school. First alert the school system that you are intending to homeschool. A NOI is required first. A Notice of Intent is simple. Just drop it off at the closest school.

To Whom It May Concern;

This Notice of Intent is to notify you that I will begin home educating my child, Emily Lynn Sanders, 5 days from today, beginning on October 1, 2012. My child is 15 years old and resides at 203 Ute Street, Kiowa, CO 80117. Mailing address is P.O. Box 2012, Elizabeth, CO 80107. The number of attendance hours this school year will be at least 688 hours.

Sincerely,   _____   Date

_____

From here, your requirements are to get them evaluated on the odd year, 5th, 7th, 9th grades, etc. There are two ways to do this. You can either subject your children to the battery test they offer at the school (which is not intended to help your child succeed. The schools get pretty upset when they lose your tax dollars for that child) or get someone to write you an evaluation. It has to be a teacher or a psychiatrist.

The first year we found a lovely lady on a homeschooling Yahoo site. I sent her the children's resume and she wrote out a statement that the children were at or above grade level. This was submitted with a copy of her teacher's license and we were free and clear for another two years. She became ill and wasn't able to help us the next time. Our lovely waitress at the bar that we shot pool at happened to be a high school teacher and was happy to evaluate the kids. I sent her their extensive resumes (you would be surprised how much your kids learn) and fifty dollars a kid and she sent in the evaluation and copy of teacher's license to the school district that we resided in.

Different Ways to Homeschool

You could choose online schooling where the children take online classes and the online school takes care of everything from NOI's to evaluations. This to me seemed not unlike the school programs I was taking them out of so I didn't opt for this course.

You could set up around the dining room table with workbooks from the teacher supply store and books and a fun teacher ledger. I tried this for four months. I enjoyed it immensely. I could make the kids read what books I found the most fascinating, had them learn all the important sciences that I deemed pertinent, and did math drills. It wasn't long before the revolt began. "This is just like school, Mom." They were unhappy. Learning is not supposed to be unhappy.

And that is when I heard of Unschooling. Sound like the kids are just running buck wild around the farm (or suburbs at the time, in our case)? They were, kind of, and learning every second of it. Once I let them have their freedom the children took on their own studies.

Shyanne became very interested in baking and spent her time reading cookbooks, writing recipes, performing fractions, halving and doubling recipes, writing grocery lists, and figuring finances to afford items.

Andrew was obsessed with music and taught himself how to play the guitar, recorder, banjo, piano, harmonica, and composed his own music and wrote poems to fit the songs. He also wrote a children's book, read everything he could on pirates, designed a board game, and completed a finance workbook for real world math.

Emily followed her siblings learning alongside them. She became interested in photography and her business, Emily's Art and Photograpy, now brings in a little extra cash.

All three kids were active at the library and in youth group. They were in a writing club and read fervently, whatever they pleased, and often at a higher grade level. They had more time to find themselves and really embrace their own passions. They can all spell, read, love history, understand science, can keep a budget, and love learning new things.

One of the benefits to homeschooling is that the children do not just interact with peers their own age. My kids have always been just as likely to befriend someone fifty years their senior as the kid next door. They have manners, we instilled what values we felt were important (of course, now as adults, they have to find their own way and ideals, but we didn't let a secular government institution decide their morals for them), and they had a great time being kids. Playing outside on nice days. Reading books in trees.

But, I warn you, children raised in this atmosphere are not followers. They do not do well working for other people their whole lives. They are ambitious, confident, entrepreneur types.

The kids can still participate in school events. Shyanne went to prom and participated in a school play. Emily participated in Cross Country Running.

Where are they now? Andrew has worked his way up through management in each job he has chosen. He concentrates on his music and performs around Denver. He is almost twenty-four years old. Shyanne is my partner at White Wolf Medicine. She also has her own bakery on the side, A Witch and a Whisk. She is twenty-one years old. Emily works for a restaurant, has her own photography company, wants to open her own restaurant, and homeschools her toddler. She is now just twenty. It may sound like a mom bragging, but my point is, I didn't screw up and you won't either!

The gist here is that if you feel that it is time to homeschool, then by all means try it. There is a learning and teaching style for everyone. For us it was running buck wild in the woods and reading books in trees.

Musings from My Homestead

I am in love with this place. It speaks to me...

of heartbreaks healed and promises kept.

The lingering wood smoke scents the air as the rustic landscape captivates me. It pulls me in and dances with me across further snowcapped peaks and nestles me near in elder Elms. I am pleased here, at peace, quiet, exhaled.

Words and new poems run through my mind- cadences and song, psalms and prayers. I think I have been burnt out for a long time. Work too hard. Expect too much of others and myself and often forget to live. The rabbit that shoots out of the brush and away in a zigzag when I startle him cares not if I answer every call or busy work myself to exhaustion. The wild world of nature will still be there if our chaos of whirlwind, human made, self-righteous living were to end. It would go on, more peacefully perhaps. I breathe again and look out across the prairie and realize my soul is connected to this natural world and I come back to myself.

The prairie is so alive. Rabbits scamper underbrush as owls speak in trees under foliage of vibrant hues. Hawks circle, the sky is huge here. Dauntingly beautiful, I cannot even find myself to paint. I could never match the beauty. Inspiration fuels me, revitalizes my senses.

Fall is evident in scenes I failed to notice in our past existence. Piles of firewood in country front yards. The thicker white coats on our goats. Chickens getting new feathers, laying less eggs. The winds are different, the clouds look different. The colors increased- vibrant, charged, glowing.

I watch for birds flying south so I have my timeline of preparedness. Firewood. Sweaters. Pantry full. Animal feed stocked. Chimney swept. Gutters cleaned. Garden prepped. Garlic planted.

My list never ends but may I learn to live in a simpler breath. Slower. Methodical. Meaningful. Breathe, the air is sweet upon us and autumn is in the air.

Wishing you all peace and inspiration on your homesteads!

Photos From the Farm

St. Francis watches over our flock.

Busy as a bee in the hive.

Elsa is a hungry girl!

Andy strumming away.

Maryjane climbing around.
What's cuter than a baby in a tree?

Baby chicks are almost as cute!

Emily and Shyanne, posing with their favorite chicken... Peep!

Have you ever seen a Colorado Sunset? Colors alive with Joy!

Hanging laundry with a wonderful view!

The beauty of a packed pantry!

Isabelle and Elsa are a big part of our pretty views.

Our Lady of the Goats.

Everybody is welcome at our Pumpkin Patch!

About the Author

Katie Sanders is a writer, teacher, herbalist, and farmer on an Urban Homestead in Pueblo, Colorado. Through her writing and business, Katie strives to encourage and inspire people of any age to pursue their dreams and live simpler. She is the founder of Garden Fairy Apothecary and the owner of White Wolf Medicine, and author of two popular blogs. When she is not gardening, teaching, or writing Katie and her husband, Doug, enjoy spending time with their three children, Andrew, Shyanne, and Emily and their granddaughter, Maryjane Rose, who is quickly becoming a farm girl and plant lover herself.

You can contact the author by sending an email to Katie@WhiteWolfHerbs.com, or by writing an old fashioned letter to P.O. Box 2012, Elizabeth, CO 80107. Check out her blogs at www.MedicineWolf.net and www.FarmGirlSchool.org. Katie is also available for speaking events.

Made in the USA
Lexington, KY
18 June 2018